THE POWER OF
GOD'S
NEGATIVES

THE POWER OF GOD'S NEGATIVES

A Contemporary Look At What God
Does Not Want Us To Do

HAROLD A. CARTER, JR.

THE POWER OF GOD'S NEGATIVES

Cover Design by Atinad Designs

© Copyright 2009

SAINT PAUL PRESS, DALLAS, TEXAS
First Printing, 2009

Unless otherwise indicated, all Scriptures are taken from the King James Version of the Holy Bible.

The name SAINT PAUL PRESS and its logo are registered as a trademark in the U.S. patent office.

ISBN-13: 978-0-9819672-8-8

Printed in the U.S.A.

"It is not only for what we do
that we are held responsible, but
also for what we do not do."

-Moliére
1622-1672

DEDICATION

To my sons:

Daniel Nathan
and
Timothy Alphonso

CONTENTS

ACKNOWLEDGMENTS

To my beloved wife, Rev. Monique T. Carter, of twenty-five blessed and joyful years of marriage and even more years of sharing and shaping my life.

To my determined father and pastor, Dr. Harold A. Carter, whose suggestions, including the fine tuning of the title, gave further dimensions to this work.

To my tireless executive secretary, Mrs. Jamelia Ward, for working through no less than a half dozen drafts.

And to my wonderful New Shiloh Church family for their ceaseless prayers and ongoing support.

FOREWORD

WEPTANOMAH DAVIS, MS
Editor, *Today's Minister's Wife Magazine*

Years of research in the field of psychology has provided answers to questions that have puzzled scientists for years. There is, however, one question that research in the field has yet to answer. Science is not able to definitively answer the question, 'What makes a person change?' How is it that one set of conditions will bring a behavior change for one person and not another? Why does one student receive a C on a test and study harder to earn an A, another student makes no changes and earns another C, and another student will say, 'why bother,' and earns a lower grade? Man's conscious ability to change has many ramifications. Imagine being able to change bad eating habits, prisoners free from recidivism and addicts free from relapse. Science knows the benefits of saying 'no' to that which harms, but getting the switch to 'click on' is the hard part. To answer this question, researchers have studied physiology, genetics, nature vs. nurture, behavior modification, punishment vs. reward, family of origin… the list goes on longer than space permits. In this book, the author, Dr. Harold Carter, Jr., has focused on the power of God's negative directives as the force for change that is needed today.

In this work, Dr. Carter considers the power of God's negative command from different perspectives. His discussion on the effects of the diminishing no's in our society is well timed when one considers the daily reports in the news on violence and corruption at every level of our culture. The author also examines the historical aspect of a negative command from God. This is excellent teaching information. At one time new believers understood that accepting Christ meant a change in behavior. This was a part of songs and testimonies. Believers would say, 'Things I used to do, I don't do no more; places I used to go, I don't go no more.' Dr. Carter reminds the reader that salvation requires being in agreement with God to say 'no' to our sinful nature. He lets us know that the purpose of salvation and our service is not for God to become a wishing well. What is of particular insight is the examination by the author that God's negative commands are the commands that free one as a Christian. One should not be in Christ unaware of how and when God calls believers to say, 'no.' Growing up, I remember hearing the phrase 'working out my soul's salvation.' Is it possible that we have lost the idea that salvation is something we work on, while we expect God to do all of the work? For many readers, this may be the first time giving serious thought to the negative aspect of God's commandments.

It is true that millions of research dollars have not been spent documenting the power of God to change lives. Indeed, mainstream research is just beginning to examine the power of spirituality and prayer. With this book, Dr. Carter has explored the power of the negative command in a format that includes his scholarship and personal reflections. Any reader will conclude that the author has taken on a weighty subject. Just as he did with volume one of *Harold's Hermeneutics,* treatment of this challenging topic is both highly readable and insightful. *The Power of God's Negatives* provides a framework to use the power of God's negative commands to change a life.

INTRODUCTION

When God created us as human beings, He gave us the wonderful gift of free will. God did not create us to be programmed like a computer. He did not insert a single "yes" or a "no" chip inside of us like a robot. God created us with the privilege to choose or, even better, the gift of choice. Because He is love, and because He loves us, it is as though He willingly takes the risk in allowing us the freedom of our will, to see if we will willingly live for him, knowing that He is our creator, redeemer, and sustainer. It is crucial, however, to know that even God's gift of free will to us has limits, blessings and consequences, depending on the choices we make. It is with this in mind that I assert that, in many ways, we have pushed the understanding of free will out of proportion.

For example, Proverbs 22:6 states, *"Train up a child in the way he (she) should go: and when he (she) is old, he (she) will not depart from it."* These words of wisdom call for parents or guardians of children to instruct, guide, discipline, and lead them by example in the way the child should go, meaning that the adult has and should have influence on the direction the child should take. For centuries, traditional families have sought to abide by this proverb, both Christian and secular. However, within the last forty to fifty years, as a result of the influences of so-called free thinking child psychologists, parents or guardians have been taught to allow their children to practically parent themselves, to become their children's friends, and given the laws in most states now, restrain from even responsible corporal punishment. Still further, parents or guardians are told to refrain from forcing their religious beliefs on their children, but allow them to develop a system of belief on their own or come to appreciate one of their own choosing.

When I was six years old, I chose to accept Jesus Christ as my personal Savior and publicly declared the same. Both of my parents are saved (albeit, my mother is now with the Lord). My grandparents on both sides of my parental tree were saved; all of whom I'd been blessed to know before they, too, went to be with the Lord. Now, did my parents or my grandparents save me or force me to be saved? Absolutely not. But, they did put me in the atmosphere to be saved. They prayed for me, took me to church, lived Christian lives, and instilled in me the Word of God. I contend that without their training me up in the way, I would not be who I am, today, by the grace of God. They allowed me to express my gift of free will, while at the same time loving me with the love of God.

Here's the point: A case can be made, especially in this Western world culture, that once the World War II generation came of age, subsequent generations that have arguably come of age based on the merits of their predecessors, have no sense of discipline, have a spirit of entitlement, and are void of any fear of God. How can they ever come back to anything if they have never been given anything to depart from in the first place? And, it is not their fault! It has been, and continues to be, the responsibility of the adults in their lives to instill in them a sense of right and wrong, and the consequences for their actions. Indeed, even free will needs boundaries. The only reason that the prodigal son was able to come to himself and subsequently return home, in Jesus' parable (St. Luke 15:11-24), was because he had left his father's house where certain values, etc., were taught. The prodigal chose to ignore them, or depart from them, only to regret having made the wrong choice, having exercised his free will.

God, in effect, says to us: "I have made you with a free will, but I will also give you training, so that you will have something to hold on to or something to come back to, even if/when you err. So, here are some things you need to know in order to help you: I don't want you to eat from this particular tree; I don't want you to have any other gods before (beside) me; I don't want you to bear false witness," and so on.

Inasmuch as God has made us who we are and has given us certain expectations of behaviors and actions that please Him, it is still our critical right of option to obey or disobey. And, interestingly, contrary to our way of thinking, many of God's expectations are couched in negative terms or language. It is what God requires of us not to do that proves our obedience to God, and when we do what we want to do, that proves our disobedience. This book will seek to explore the power of choosing no, for there is much to be said that our no leads to our being blessed, while our yes leads to our being cursed.

-Dr. Harold A. Carter, Jr.
Baltimore, Maryland

"For since the beginning of the world men have not heard, nor perceived by the ear, neither hath the eye seen, O God, beside thee, what he hath prepared for him that waiteth for him."

-Isaiah 64:4

PART ONE

NEGATIVITY:
BIBLICAL,
FOUNDATIONAL,
AND PSYCHOLOGICAL

CHAPTER ONE

NEGATIVITY AND GOD'S LAW

The moral and civil regulations and laws that most, if not all, major world religions, as well as the foundation of most civilized systems of juris prudence, can be traced to the decalogue, or what has commonly come to be known as The Ten Commandments. "The Ten Commandments tell us what not to do. Even the two that are stated positively, Sabbath observance and honoring, can easily be put in negative form like the others—and perhaps they were originally negative in form too."[1]

There are two universally accepted distinct types of law, based on their intended purposes. There is case law and there is categorical law. Case law is generally developed over time as the result of decisions of judges and/or "long-tested experience handed down over generations." The Ten Commandments are not case laws, they are categorical laws. Categorical laws "flatly assert actions that are not to be taken under any circumstances. But, the Ten Commandments are much more than categorical law. They are more basic. They provide no penalties, and therefore make clear then these laws are not like other categorical laws that specify punishment. The Ten Commandments are foundational, the groundwork for the laws that are to guide Israel and humankind generally."[2] From the spiritual and biblical point of view, the law is purely theocratic, meaning that it comes from God and not from humans. In terms of God's law, most would agree that the law breaks down into even more specified categories such as: Civil, Criminal, Judicial, Constitutional, Ecclesiastical, and Ceremonial.

During the last century and a half, many law collections have been discovered in the Middle East. The most famous, of course, is the Code of Hammurabi, but there are also law collections of the Assyrians and the Hittites, among others. The law collections have many similarities to the laws found in parts of the books of Exodus, Leviticus, Numbers, and Deuteronomy. There are no parts, however, that very closely resemble the Ten Commandments in form or in content.

The first five books of the Old Testament, said to have been written by Moses, are replete with more than six hundred regulations and laws, ranging from what to eat, to how to offer proper sacrifices, to how to dress for ceremonies. Yet, they all have their basic and fundamental essence in the holy writings written with the very finger of God upon the stone tablets carried down from Mt. Sinai by Moses for the purpose of being lived out by the Hebrews, who had only recently been set free from the laws of the land of Egyptian and "pharo-saic" tyranny and oppression; laws that kept them enslaved, oppressed, and bound. Now, the God Who had given them their freedom was giving them new laws to live by. If it was under their former system that they found themselves enslaved by the law, it seems only reasonably right that God's system of law would be for them a system of liberation. Laws and regulations were still necessary but God's law precipitated and operated out of love, not tyranny.

The Ten Commandments and the laws of the Books of Moses, also known as the Torah and the Pentateuch, were not the first laws of God. The creation narratives of Genesis 1 and 2 indicate that after God created Adam (1:26; 2:7) and Eve (1:27; 2:21-22), the first man and the first wo-man (man with a womb), that He gave them dominion over the created things on the earth, the gift of nomenclature of those created things, the blessing of fertility and procreation, and the joy of sublime intimacy and innocence with Him and with each other (1:28; 2:8, 18-25), then, He also, gave them a prohibition.

It is in the context of these narratives that bespeak the creative work and will of God's enormous compassion, generosity, and excellence, all of which are exemplified by the tremendous sense of implicit freedom that Adam and Eve were given, generally referred to by theologians as free will, that God instituted a signal way to have Adam and Eve affirm His sovereignty. In essence, Adam and Eve had it made. Their Creator had made them. Their Creator had made things for them. And, their Creator had given them the gift to make more of themselves. However, lest they should lose sight of the source of all they were made to enjoy and appreciate, ultimately inclusive of their Creator, Genesis 2:16-17 indicates that God said to Adam: "… *of every tree of the garden thou mayest freely eat: But of the tree of the knowledge of good and evil, thou shalt not eat of it: for in the day that thou eatest thereof thou shalt surely die.*"

The inspiration for this book is rather simple. It is generated out of the spirit of the Genesis 2:17 and Exodus 20:1-17 prohibitions that project successful moral, civil, and spiritual living based on what not to do. It is as the result of what not to do as God's created beings, and descendants of Adam and Eve that we please God and avoid the consequences of displeasing God. Granted, there are a plethora of things to do—worship, discipleship, stewardship, etc. However, arguably, the cord that holds the God-human relationship together can be traced to affirming the sovereignty of God by not disobeying Him (His command/commands). The idea that Adam and Eve were not to eat from one particular tree was God's way of saying to them that he owned everything. Every time they would see that tree, they would be reminded of God's ownership. To deliberately eat from it was an ultimate insult against God's ownership, and even His sovereignty.

Parenthetically, one of the ways to appreciate the basis of God's creation is from the perspective of reversal. We know that Genesis means "beginning," and therefore the Bible takes the reader on a journey from the beginning to the ending, known and described as the Revelation. If, indeed, the Revelation is about God's created beings ultimately being with Him, albeit redeemed and glorified, would not such be a state of a new beginning? What appears to be an ending is actually a beginning.

Still further, note a tradition that the Hebrews (Jews, if you will) have embraced since creation, although the Gentiles have reversed it. In Genesis 1:5, after God is described as dividing the light from the darkness, and calling the light day and the darkness night, there is this line: *"And the evening and the morning were the first day."* This sequence is repeated five more times, at the end of each subsequent day, save the seventh day, the day

God is described as having completed His work of creation, and therefore rested.

Interestingly, over and against our traditional and contemporary perspective that has our day starting in the morning and ending in the evening, the original perspective, and perhaps the correct perspective, is to view the day starting in the evening and ending in the morning. After all, it is this perspective that rightfully helps us to view the resurrection of Jesus, the Son of God, as having been raised "on the third day." Based on our gentile understanding of a day, we are hard pressed to come up with "the first day of the week" (ref. John. 20:1) as being the third day from Friday given that Jesus died Friday at 3:00 p.m. Technically, less than two days or less than 48 hours, would have passed from Friday afternoon until Sunday morning, given our timetable. However, given the Genesis perspective, Jesus' death would have occurred at the end of the first day, Friday afternoon. From Friday evening to Saturday evening would have been the second day. Saturday evening would have been the beginning of the third day, making Sunday morning the apex or center of the third day. Jesus rose in the morning, the middle, the summit, the peak, and the center of the chiasm of the third day that started with evening, not morning.

God established the fundamental and foundational systems for our good. He is using what we deem to be negative, and ironically, although the language is, our adherence to it will prove to be positive. We have flipped the script by seeing God's prohibitions or negatives as negative. The reality is that when we are obedient to God's "thou shalt nots" we maintain our liberty, purpose, and relationship. It is adhering to the nots that give us life, even life abundantly. It is violating them that gives us something much less, even death.

Whatever else we might do, God's "thou shalt nots" command us, "do not do these things, and we will be all right." We are commanded to acquire an understanding of things that we should dare not do, must not do, or we or our community will suffer the consequences. Each one of us, as well as our respective communities need to know "almost instinctively that there are some things that simply are not done."[3]

Consequently, the negativity of the law, albeit God's law, sets the parameter, establishes the boundary, and determines the expectations based upon what the Hebrews, as well as ourselves, are not to do. God is operating out of negative discipline or enforcement. Negative discipline or enforcement is the implied warning of suffering that results as the consequence of bad behavior. Most of us are acquainted with negative reinforcement—a concept researched by B. F. Skinner, devised to guide a person to the appropriate action in order to avoid unwarranted consequences. Negative reinforcement strengthens a behavior because a negative condition is stopped or avoided as a consequence of the behavior. However, when there is an adherence to negative enforcement, the reinforcement is not necessary. It is instruction from the bottom up and not from the top down and thereby eliminates any excuse of, "but, I didn't know that I wasn't supposed to," or "couldn't do." It's really masterful, for most are prone to look for loopholes and exceptions. "Don't" and "not" eliminate loopholes. The negativity focuses on an issue or area. "The negative form actually helps, for it does not give a specific definition; rather, it describes an area that must be avoided."[4] Hence, God's laws have their basis in the language of "thou shalt not" and inextricably lead us into the power of additional biblical negatives.

CHAPTER TWO

NEGATIVITY AND EVOLUTION IN BRIEF

Most of us would prefer not to be around negativity, especially negative people. Negative people have negative attitudes and/or speak negatively about almost everything. They don't think the project can be done. They refuse to believe their friend's marriage will last. They can never appreciate any kind of weather, even if it's 70° and the sky is blue. And, they have a way of finding fault in everyone, but (of course) themselves.

I confess that I have been known to be a little too observant, a bit of a complainer, a lover of understatements, and often display a rather dark sense of humor. But, I am a believer, and to be a believer demands a positive attitude and/or positive speech. Personally, people who are negative probably have had or have some kind of faith crisis, for Christianity calls us to accept and believe that all things are possible, or more accurately, *"… with God nothing shall be impossible"* (St. Luke 1:37). Reality would have it that as Christians we will have moments of "why me," doubt, fear, and ifs, but our faith and belief in God should always override any negativity and prevail time after time. There is no need to constantly remain negative when one has God. "Misery (negativity) loves company," and that kind of company, I don't need.

The term negativity, where humans are concerned, refers to the tendency of some people to assign more negative weight to information in descriptions of others or events.[1] And I have found that negative people aren't just satisfied simply being negative in describing people or things that may or may not be negative, but because they're negative people, they will also amplify what they're describing as negative or more negative.

Negativity is real. And, typically it is something that most of us prefer not to have to deal with. We don't like negative or bad news. We don't like negative results or outcomes. We don't like losing, failure, or defeat because they're all associated with negativity. However, the fact-of-the-matter is, negativity is a part of life, and it impacts us. Bad things happen. Evil exists.

Recent psychological studies even indicate, "events that are negatively valenced (e.g. losing money, being abandoned by friends, and receiving criticism) will have a greater impact on (an) individual than positively valenced events of the same type (e.g. winning money, gaining friends, and receiving praise)."[2] This suggests that we are more affected by negative events than positive events. Even if such is not the case, negative events have a high degree of importance in our lives. Still further:

> The greater power of bad events over good ones in everyday events, major life events (e.g. trauma) close

> relationship outcomes, social network patterns,
> interpersonal interactions, and leaving processes. Bad
> (negative) emotions, bad parents, and bad feedback have
> more impact than good ones, and bad information is
> processed more thoroughly than good....
>
> Findings suggest that bad is stronger than good as a
> general principle across a broad range of psychological
> phenomena.[3]

Needless to say, the preceding findings must be kept in proper
perspective. The point being, however, that negativity has
tremendous weight on our psyches. The average news producers
have known this for decades: bad news sells. We buy in (no pun
intended) to fires, kidnappings, home invasions, political
upheavals, and gossip.

History has also demonstrated that negativity seems to prevail.
One may even dare say, "it's evolutionary." Think about it this
way: we've been taught and conditioned that "only the strong
survive." By strong, the suggestion is, the species that has the
ability to dominate, if not destroy, other weaker and less efficient
species. Such is also referred to as, "Survival of the fittest," not
to also mention the saying "Good guys finish last." I recognize
and accept that nature has a certain built-in cycle that sends the
message, "might prevails over right," and we must accept that,
where nature is concerned, such is a part of the natural order
of things.

While listening to Maryland Public Radio recently, I heard an
interview between the host, Marc Steiner, and a California
physician, Dr. Peter Wybrow. Dr. Wybrow has written a book

entitled, *When More Is Not Enough.* The reason for the interview had to do, however, with an article that the doctor published entitled "Dangerously Addictive." He makes the case that as humans, we are paleolithic creatures having evolved over millions of years, but it has only been the last 100,000 years that we have emerged from a reptilian brain to a "rational/executive mind" due to the development of our frontal cortex. It is our frontal cortex that gives us the capability for long term planning and abstract thinking, but (and this is the point) fundamentally we have been creatures of immediacy, self-interest, and greed. Essentially, ours has been a plight of self-survival.

Given our nation's and our world's current economic travail, even if one doesn't believe in Darwinism, let alone evolution, that even when we consider Adam and Eve's disobedience and selfishness, it would seem that although we're in the 21st century that we haven't evolved that much. Dr. Wybrow indicated that we cannot resist (we cannot say, "no" to) the "short term," especially when it's in front of us (i.e. food, money, etc.); that we prefer to indulge our curiosity. And, so, he raised the question, "Are we biologically suited for consumerism? What the discussion was getting at is the need for humans to be mindful of our baser beginnings and instincts and strive towards a greater social behavior in order to attain balance. We cannot civilly survive living out the "crabs in a barrel" concept. Ours must be to take full advantage of the part of our brain—that frontal cortex—and apply it to an even greater extent, lest we miss out on long term gains for short term failures. Negative people are essentially negative people because they've yet to open their minds to greater, more hopeful and optimistic possibilities. Here, we are not talking about wishful thinking or fantasy. We're talking about faith for today and for the future that there is "enough" for all. There's no need to be negative, in this vein, because God has blessings, and then some.

Mine is not to debate this argument that negativity, whether in our personal or communal lives, or in nature, is stronger than positivity. I certainly don't believe, morally or spiritually, that evil wins out over good. My aim is to raise the awareness that negativity has in our lives, especially in our spiritual lives, and when used effectively—even as God does—it can be extremely valuable, beneficial, and prove to be positive!

I thought that I would, at least, share a brief word acknowledging the normal and traditional understanding of negativity, because the preceding understanding is not the essence of my focus. If, indeed, we can start with the belief that God is creator of all, then we have to accept that He made both that which is positive and that which is negative, the good and the bad. Still further, we must accept that since God is God that He can use both as He sees fit. Ours then is to seek to get a handle on God's usage of negativity for our good and for our benefit. If God can bless us on the mountain, God can bless us in the valley…perhaps, even more so.

CHAPTER THREE

NEGATIVITY AND SLOWING THINGS DOWN

In many ways, negativity is a refusal. It is a refusal to entertain, consider, or accept. It is a cancellation or a removal. Often, negativity is associated with pessimism; however, negativity does not have to be associated with a lack of hope, usually associated with pessimism. To refuse a certain invitation, opportunity, or chance is by no means pessimistic or an attitude of hopelessness. In fact, as opposed to closing the door on hope, a refusal may be the best way of opening the door on hope. In actuality, hope has occurred, because the negativity has proven to be positive, beneficial, optimistic, and liberating.

Look back over your life, and recall the incident, or incidents, that seemed rather enticing to you. In spite of the allure, if not possible thrill of the enticement, you refused to engage in the same. In retrospect, you have come to realize that to have been positive by accepting would have been the wrong thing to have been. Your "yes" would have led to real problems and consequences that would have altered your life, whereas your "no," as difficult as it may have been, set you (if not made you) free.

Several months prior to my leaving my second pastorate, in Petersburg, Virginia, a somewhat distant member of the church contacted the office in order to indicate that he wanted to schedule pre-marital counseling, as well as a date for his marriage. When the pre-marital session began, obviously I had the chance to meet his bride-to-be, who was not a member of that church. Both of them were in their early 40s, and it was for him, his second marriage.

As the session progressed, he began to share more and more of his expectations, revealing deep chauvinism. Even though, these were grown adults and had known each other through work for a number of years, the woman's reaction was utter shock, and she noticeably recoiled in her seat. At that time, I had been pastoring for almost thirteen years and, in spite of obvious signs of potential trouble of one kind or another, nothing had ever convinced me to come right out and advise a couple to reconsider... until that day. He scared me, and I can only imagine what his fiancé was going through.

The day before I left Petersburg to move back to Baltimore, I was packing the last few things from my office at the church into my trunk, when a car pulled up onto the parking lot. Out jumped the woman with a box that she said she wanted me to open in her presence. It was a plaque which she'd had engraved thanking me for saving her from that marriage. The ultimate no, which was once even a yes, I'm sure was difficult, but kept her free. Deciding to say no made her grateful.

Negativity, then, is really an act of opposition. The refusal is the result of what is felt, thought, and/or believed. When met with anti-feelings, thoughts, and/or beliefs, we process the information and take an opposite stand from what is offered. Granted, the word "opposition" has been given a bad connotation, as in the "opposition forces" primarily because we have been taught and conditioned to connect "opposition" with bad, wrong, and even evil. Interestingly, the word "opposite" is not as threatening. Indeed, opposite suggests a counter balance and not a counter evil.

Essentially, opposition and opposite are one and the same, and negativity then is essentially the counter balance of that which is anti. Negativity, is therefore, good, healthy, and sensible, for it ensures that we will not be blindly led without processing the information and run the risk of making the wrong choice, although it looks and appears "right."

A cousin of pessimism, but with major distinctions, is skepticism. Negativity needs skepticism in order to carry out the processing of information. How many times have we heard, "Not everything that looks good on the outside will be good for you?" The way of determining the benefit of what will be good is by not leaping into circumstances without processing, analyzing, and examining. Many times we respond based on a gut feeling, discernment, and conscience; all of which, I profess, is God-talk or God-led. Notwithstanding, it is the initial action of skepticism that slows everything (the process) down, allowing for the perspective of skepticism to take place.

Skepticism is having a questioning attitude, and questioning needs time. Many a yes would have been a no, if we only took or made time to question what was being asked or what we were about to get ourselves into. The proverbial statement "haste makes waste" has much merit. Peer pressure and sexual encounters are such nemesis because they usually devalue time. "Don't miss out on this. The moment is right, now. C'mon, while we have a chance," are typical lines of the language used to mitigate against making time to question what needs to be questioned. We must teach ourselves to slow our response down.

> "Many times we launch out on our own and end up stepping on a landmine because we fail to consider God's might and promises. Instead we mentally rush past evidences of His faithfulness… and move forward without consulting Him about the future. When we make a conscious decision to bypass God and His principles, we make a horrendous mistake."[1]

Negativity, then, can be seen as our warning system, in addition to serving as our boundary (as will be discussed in chapter 4). A warning is posted or sounded essentially for our safety. Alarms, signs, and advice are all for the benefit of our well being. The tragedy, of course, is when we don't heed motherly advice, warning us that if we play with fire, we will get burned. There is a certain amount of training and learning by falling and getting back up that comes with the maturation process. However, once we are able to stand maturely, on our own two feet, why are we still willing to take risks and ignore the warnings that are clearly evident? "No swimming." "The Surgeon General's Warning: Smoking Causes Lung Cancer, Heart Disease, Emphysema, etc." Yet, we still take our liberty to do what we please, almost exclusively aware of the consequences. Somehow, we talk ourselves into thinking or believing that we will be the one who will somehow be the exception by avoiding the danger, not getting caught, not becoming sick, not ruining our reputation, and so on.

In many ways, due to civilization's ongoing evolution of sophistication we have become emboldened with time. As a result, we have lost an enormous amount of innocence, if not also the better part of naivety. I dare not suggest that we turn back the hand of time to the Stone Age, Puritanism, or to the black and white days of television, but those ages of so much "unknown," as well as enforced standards kept a lot of people out of trouble and saved a lot of lives. Even when we compare our Western culture to some less sophisticated Eastern cultures, from our perspective, we find ourselves poking fun at their so-called standards, laws, and religious practices, while we boast about our free society, liberality, transparency, and all the while we're participating in the demise of our own culture. More and more, we have become exhibitionists and have lost the notion of "you can't do wrong and get by." Sex sells, anything goes, and "don't hold back," are truly symptomatic calling cards of our boldness to do as we please.

We have all but concluded that a person can commit the most heinous of crimes and get by. And until recently, such boldness gave carte blanche to mortgage companies, insurance companies, brokerage firms, and Wall Street. Again, this "pushing the envelope" has become practically how we live in almost every aspect of our society, including the church. When was the last time you heard "you can't do wrong and get by" from the pulpit, or when was the last time you heard about hypocritical living— saying or professing one thing but doing another? Oddly enough, the world of politics may be the last bastion of accountability and, of course, politics has always been and always will be, partisan (which, in my view is window dressing), but at least our representatives play the role of accountability.

The reality seems to be that we have become emboldened, because we no longer have prophets—prophets in the biblio-classical sense. We have dumbed down the warning associated with God's Word, and therefore relegated the "fire and brimstone" message as irrelevant. If our present level of faith has little or no aspect of consequence, then our system of juris prudence has little or no underpinnings, our communities and our society degrade into anarchy, and we as individuals end up with little or no integrity.

The absence of the prophet whose message agitated, convicted, and challenged lifestyles, systems, and empires may have seemed ineffective and defeatist, but it gave definition, or sides, to life. There was God's way, and there was Satan's way. There was a right way, and there was a wrong way. The silence of such a message has allowed for a blurring of the sides and a graying of the colors. If nothing else, the prophet kept tension and agitation in the hearts of people, as well as in the community, and that is always healthy.

It was/is the message of the prophet that calls us to question and think twice, slowing the process down. It was/is the message of the prophet that conveys hope through obedience to God. It was/is the message of the prophet that distinguished and clarified God's expectations as opposed to our desires.

In the absence of such, a communal, national, or universal spokesperson, or spokespersons, might I postulate that we return to an emphasis on our conscience. Almost never, do we hear anyone referring to their conscience as their guide, anymore. The likelihood is that inasmuch as the external prophet had been muted, the same has all but occurred to our conscience, or what I will call our internal prophet. Although, as I have previously alluded, I contend that such an inner faculty or voice is the God in us, our societal mentors (parents, teachers, pastors, police, officers of the courts, etc.) have had little to say to this present, or even the previous, generation, in this regard. Again, Proverbs 22:6 instructs: *"Train up a child in the way he/she should go, and when he/she is old he/she will not depart from it."* The onus is not on the child to be somehow trained on their own or through osmosis. The onus is on the ones who are to do the training.

> … The disrespect that we see being expressed by young people all over the world is rooted in how children have been mistreated, miseducated, misdirected and unloved as infants and toddlers… the blame should not be put on the children for the way they are behaving. But instead grown ups should look into their own hearts, homes, and churches, where children have been devalued and segregated as second-class citizens… All…are profoundly affected by the adults that they come into contact with when they are children. We must never underestimate the impact that we have upon the mental sky of children…[2]

How we impact our children is tremendously crucial. A lot of emphasis on how we act is usually stressed, and rightly so. It should, however, not mitigate against the power of what we say. We are losing generations because we have practically stopped using crucial language that instills in our children the value of listening to their conscience, if not at least using—and here is another all but passé term—common sense.

Conscience, common sense, inner voice, and so on gave our predecessors warning, and even when they unfortunately did not listen, the proceeding led to guilt and/or regret. (I know. What are they?) At the very least, when we mess up, fail, make the wrong decision, and sin, shouldn't we be remorseful? Watch some of the court dramas and trials. Observe some of the reports featuring criminal behavior. You will see a certain detachment, if not arrogance. Have we become pathological as a society? Have we become sociopaths?

The fact-of-the-matter is, in many ways, we have inverted our standards. The "gangsta" has been glorified, and the honorable has been humiliated. During one of the inaugural balls held in honor of Barack Obama's election as our country's 44th president, singer and entertainer Beyoncé Knowles, serenaded our nation's first couple, singing "At Last," as they majestically danced. The nation, nor the world, had ever seen anything like it, before. It was a magical day, a magical evening, and a magical moment. Truly, history had been and was being made.

The next day on the Tom Joyner Morning Show, a popular syndicated radio show, the comedian "Earthquake" observed the following: "Do ya'll know why Beyoncé was crying while she was singing? Those weren't tears of joy over President Obama's historical election. Those were tears of regret. She was singing and looking at Barack and Michelle, and it dawned on her that she was married to a gangsta, but Michelle was married to a Harvard scholar. She was crying because the day of the gangsta was over and the day of the scholar had dawned."

Granted, it is the comedian's job to find humor, even at the risk of audience feedback, considering Beyoncé's husband, Sean Carter (aka Jay Z) took the gangsta image and parlayed it all the way to the top of the Hip Hop industry, having been the CEO of Def Jam Recording and Roc-A-Fella Records. Presently, he is pursuing various business ventures, inclusive of being a co-owner of the New Jersey Nets.

Anyone with a sense of history and pride was certainly swept up emotionally; yet, with all due respect, could it be that through "Earthquake's" comedic lenses, we are seeing a reversal of the reversal? Are we righting the ship after all of its flipping? Only time will tell. Yet, having inverted so many of our standards, we have all but eliminated or muted a sense of right and wrong.

The 82 year old Baltimore former attorney, George L. Russell, Jr., who advocated for political, social, and civic causes said, while sharing during a luncheon meeting at our church that shame and guilt are no longer a part of many of our young people's thinking when they do wrong. He went on to reminisce about his youth, stating what many of his generation experienced, "As a result of integration, we lost our sense of community. When I did wrong, as a youth, I was not only held accountable by my parents, but by my neighbors, teachers, anyone…I knew what shame and guilt were."

Dr. Gardner C. Taylor, retired pastor of the Concord Baptist Church, Brooklyn, NY, and often referred to as the "Dean of Black Preachers," said that he once heard a man say that he was not ashamed of anything he had ever done. To which Dr. Taylor responded, "That's about all I am, is 'a-shame'." The absence of guilt has enormous implications. We don't have to be sorry for what we have done. Forget being responsible for our own actions, or accountable for what we have done. We have become experts at denial and professionals at passing blame. But there is a God; a God who does hold us accountable; and, although Adam and Eve tried their best to hide and pass blame, the looming question from God was, "... *where art thou?*" (Genesis 3:9). Only a few moments earlier they were naked and not ashamed (2:25). A few moments later, they were hiding, only to eventually pass blame and suffer the consequences of their impulsive actions. If Adam and Eve had only refused. If they had only slowed things down. If they had only acted by accepting the negativity of God's command.

One of the basic laws of mathematics is that two negatives create a positive. God's prohibition was *"thou shalt not eat of the tree...."* All Eve, and subsequently Adam had to do would have been to refuse the words of the serpent (Genesis 3:1), and the cancellation of the consequences would have been in effect, thereby leaving a positive result. "Had Adam and Eve said 'No' to the serpent, in effect, they would have been saying 'Yes' to God."[3]

CHAPTER FOUR

NEGATIVITY AND THE ONE WORD BOUNDARY

As a college student at Eastern College (now Eastern University), in St. Davids, Pennsylvania, during the early 1980's, I recall that Ronald Reagan was our country's president. During the years of his administration, while he was talking "trickle down economics" and "reaganomics," his wife, Nancy Reagan, chose to lend her role as First Lady to the so-called "War On Drugs" with particular focus on youth. The campaign's catch phrase was, "Just say, no." Many pundits dismissed her campaign as too simplistic and shallow; after all, can impressionable teenagers and young people just saying "no" fight off the luring temptation from family or friends who use drugs, from the pressure of peers partying on weekends, or from cunning dealers?

To be sure, there is a segment of humanity that can claim the benefit of possessing unwavering resistance (moral fiber, inner strength, and will power). They don't even have to say, "no." They just won't and don't. Let us refer to those who have such resistance as being hard wired. Might I also include in this grouping those who have will power to break habits or addictions, as well as change their direction or course from an adverse direction, once they've discovered the same to be detrimental. The late Dr. William A. Jones, Jr., who pastored the Bethany Baptist Church, Brooklyn, NY and was one of my father's closest friends, would often tell how he stopped smoking, a vice that he'd enjoyed over many years. As he had lit up, one day, while driving one of his daughters, Jennifer, home from school, she began to lecture him about the dangers of smoking which she'd learned in Health class. He continued to puff away, until she commented in a rather resigned, yet serious, tone "Ah, Daddy, you just don't have any will power." He promptly extinguished his lit cigarette and threw the rest of the pack out of the window, and that was that.

However, there is another segment that even if or when they say "no," are unable to maintain that stance, due to curiosity, lack of will power, and plain old temptation. They would be loose-wired. On the one hand, Nancy Reagan's catch phrase has merit, but only for those with the wiring (or will) to hold forth. On the other hand, for others, just saying "no," in and of itself, frankly speaking, is somewhat of a joke. Something must substantively back up the "no."

Our "no" should ideally be used, especially in important and critically decisive moments, as a way by which we can honor and please God. Based on what God would have us do, as well as not do, ours is to please Him through the respect and obedience of His will and word. When we are faced with decisions, regardless of type or degree, we must resist the desire to even compromise and say no, knowing that not only is our no the right thing to do, but it is also the righteous thing to do. It should be our desire to avoid or not to do a lot of things simply because not doing them honors God. Adam Hamilton writes in his book entitled, *Seeing Gray In A World of Black and White*: "There are courses of action I take in my life with an eye towards honoring God and expressing my love and devotion to him, though they have no direct bearing good or bad (on others). (For example) Every morning as I begin my day (I just don't head straight to the shower), but I slip to my knees next to my bed and pray."[1] I take Hamilton to mean that he tries not to take God for granted.

We have been taught to fear God, in the sense of believing that He will punish us for our disobedience, (as will even be discussed in the next chapter). However, when it comes to honoring God, pleasing God, and respecting God, based on our obedience there's a strange silence. Actually, what we seem to have done is profess worship and praise as substitutes for obedience and faithfulness. But, "obedience (to obey) is better than sacrifice"— another word for worship (I Sam. 15:22), and "Without faith it is impossible to please him" (Hebrews 11:6). Our honoring God ought to be our ultimate boundary.

Enticements and temptations can only be avoided when boundaries are implemented and utilized. By definition, boundaries, or a boundary, is a limit or limitation. A limit or limitation, for our purpose, is a line or point beyond which someone or something cannot or may not proceed. Likewise, "no" represents a choice. It is also indicative of an end. To say "no" and be effective is to establish and keep boundaries.

In the book, *Boundaries*, Dr. Henry Cloud and Dr. John Townsend call no, "The One-Word Boundary."[2] It is usually the first word associated with boundaries we learn to use. Arguably, the word "mine,"—often our first spoken word—has a certain orientation in selfishness that may be seen too as a boundary. However, the word no is much more definitive." Cloud and Townsend introduce their discussion of The One-Word Boundary in a section of their book discussing the development of boundaries entitled, "Rapprochement: I Can't Do Everything."

> Rapprochement, which occurs from around eighteen months to three years, comes from a French word meaning "a restoration of harmonious relations."

> In other words, the child comes back to reality. The grandiosity of the past few months slowly gives way to the realization that "I can't do everything I want."[3]

In addition to anger and ownership, No: The One-Word Boundary, is a tool we learn to use, early on, to build boundaries. "Toddlers going through rapprochement frequently use one of the most important words in the human language: the word no."[4] Cloud and Townsend go on to state, "The word no helps children separate from what they don't like. It gives them the power to make choices. It protects them."[5]

If a satisfactory case can be made for no as one of our successful early developmental boundaries, then it should follow that its maintenance should be preserved. Most of us have heard people say, or we ourselves say, "I just don't know how to say, 'no.'" Or, we know people who are, or we ourselves are, "yes people." Such persons are givers, supporters, and optimistic. They are also often associated with being weak, spineless, or not having any backbone. "Nothing spreads you thinner than trying to please everyone," writes Amanda Hinnant in an article "10 Ways to Say No, Guilt-Free." "Thinking you are a bad person is a symptom of 'the disease to please.'"[6] Somehow and somewhere, a lack of establishing and/or maintaining the important concept of no got lost.

Cloud and Townsend tell the story of one of their male clients who had difficulty refusing his wife's constant demands, causing him to almost go broke, trying to keep up with the Joneses. He shared that he was the youngest of four children and the only boy. Until he was in the sixth grade, his older sisters were bigger and stronger. They would take advantage of their size and beat him until he was bruised.

He was puzzled because of the attitude his parents had enforcing the teaching that boys don't hit girls and to do so was bad manners. He was taught that he had to take it, and his parents were complicit in his not being able to defend himself.[7] Neither Cloud, Townsend, or I are suggesting that he was to physically fight back; however, his parents should have established boundaries equally for his sisters, as well as for themselves. Whether they recognized it, or not, they sent the signal to their son that he had to take it, even if it hurt him physically. He, nor they, said "no." As a result, "Blocking a child's ability to say no handicaps that child for life. Adults with handicaps like (this) boundary injury: they say yes to bad thing. ...The inability to say no to the bad (becomes) pervasive."[8]

When people come of age without the ability to say no when necessary, they often end up in dangerous or abusive relationships. This type of boundary problem (often) paralyzes people's no muscles.[9] Very often, opportunities develop for people to safely vent, disclose, and open-up, but they avoid the same, in essence saying no to the possibility for help and therefore remaining in a condition or conditions that often are prone to be difficult and unhealthy.

> At the heart of the struggle is a confusion of boundaries as walls. Boundaries are supposed to be able to "breathe," to be like fences with a gate that can let the good in and the bad out. Individuals with walls for boundaries can let in neither bad nor good.

> God designed our personal boundaries to have gates. We should have the freedom to enjoy safe relationships and to avoid destructive ones. God even allows us the freedom to let Him in or to close him off: *"Here I am! I stand at the door (the gate) and knock. If anyone hears my voice and opens the door, I will come in and eat with him, and he with me."* (Rev.3:20)[10]

To the extreme, there are no addicts. These are people who started out using no and have come of age still using nothing else but no. We don't want to become no addicts, but when experience proves that no works, no will be easier the next time. The point is that clearly no must come to be appreciated and respected. It is to be used for our protection and security, but not as a security blanket. Remember, Cloud and Townsend head their section, "I Can't Do Everything." No should never be used exclusively. There are some things we can do, need to do, and must do.

Again, almost all of us have had difficulty saying no. We are not all hard-wired, or have the greatest of will power. Most of us have to first acknowledge that it's OK to say no, and we must seek to maintain the proper usage of this One-Word Boundary. Perhaps Nancy Reagan was on to something with her "War On Drugs" catch phrase: "Just say, no," especially when it is backed up with the understanding that we are honoring God, and enforcing our boundary (boundaries), even as God asks and expects us to enforce His.

The Apostle Paul, in Romans 6, was struggling to get a handle on his salvation in conjunction with temptations he was fighting. He knew he was saved, but he did not fully understand his Christian experience. The very thing he wished to do, namely, good, he did not do, and the very thing he did not want to do, namely, sin, he did do. "He was struggling in his own strength to keep from sinning and to do what was right...Many Christians are in a like situation.[11] Without a doubt, boundaries help in assisting us in being able to say, "no," but there is no greater assistance than our faith and the strength it gives us.

> The truth in Romans 6 enables the believer to gain consistent victory (in being able to say, "no." The first fact that Paul brings out is that (our) sinful nature has had its power over the believer broken. The believer before salvation was absolutely the slave of the evil nature. But since grace has separated him from its power, he does not need to obey it. When he learns this, he learns that he has the power to say a point blank NO to it. This is one great step in the battle...And the beautiful thing about it all is that the more he says NO to it, the easier it is to withstand it, until it becomes a habit...Thus, it is a matter of breaking the bad habit of saying YES to

the evil nature and forming the good habit of saying NO.[12]

"The power of that word No is crucial in the development of human character...(We) have not developed in our day that proper respect for (the) word No. The struggle to say No is difficult because human creatures always feel like the answer means losing something...Nonetheless, the biblical record makes clear that 'No' is a mighty affirmation when said to uphold the principle of God's Word...A positive 'No' always affirms a mighty 'Yes'![13]

CHAPTER FIVE

NEGATIVITY AND GOD'S STOP SIGN

Being told what not to do has a unique way of causing, if not forcing, us to deal with the very foundation of what we have been told, or asked not to do. When my mother told me, in spite of having been invited, that I could not go to a certain high school classmates' party, it caused me to think about who exactly was this classmate? What might happen at a party that my classmate was going to have? Why would the classmate want me to be at their party? And, who else had been invited? Certainly, I was initially disappointed, probably pouted, and probably had an attitude, but deep, down inside, I sensed that maybe, just maybe, Momma knew best.

Similarly, when God tells us "not to," it causes us to actually think, why would God not want us to do something? Why shouldn't we eat of the tree of the knowledge of good and evil? Why should we have no other gods before/besides God? Why shouldn't we steal, commit adultery, or lie? I contend that when we honestly consider what God is telling or asking us not to do, and we don't do it, that a certain spiritual harmony is maintained. Our obedience to God gives us peace, our relationships with others remain intact, and the spirit realm is at rest. It is as though, after we've given the situation proper consideration, a certain relief, if not peace ensues. We really don't want to live under the pressure of looking over our shoulders wondering if our misdeeds will catch up to us, or kicking ourselves for not looking at all angles before we acted. Speaking further about this, Harrelson writes, "What the commandments do is affirm that a wholesome life in communion with God and with one's fellow human beings is endangered if these prohibitions are violated."[1]

Violations are detrimental. Any form of unwanted and/or unwarranted penetration is harmful; harmful for the person or object and harmful to society and the spiritual atmosphere. When the Fall occurred in Genesis three, Eve's, and subsequently Adam's, disobedience not only led to their own punishment, but their surroundings also bore the punishment of their actions. God dispersed such punishments as curses, enmity, sorrow, bruising, joyless labor, and spiritual death, respective to Adam, Eve, and the serpent. Moreover, as the father and mother of the human race, their violation of God's command still affects us 6,000 years later as we are still the inheritors of what theologians call the "Adamic nature;" meaning, that even if we never actively sin by stealing or telling a lie, that simply by our having been born, we have a sinful nature, and are therefore sinners.

The Scriptures are very clear as to the identity of the evil (or Adamic) nature which indwells an individual as he is born into this world. One only has to glance at such portions as the following, in order to appraise the character of this sinful nature: *"And God saw that the wickedness of man was great on the earth, and that every imagination of the thoughts of his heart was only evil continually."* (Genesis 6:5): *"There is none righteous, no, not one; there is none that understandeth, there is none that seeketh after God. They are all gone out of the way, they are together become unprofitable; there is none that doeth good, no, not one"* (Romans 3:10-12). The Bible has thus isolated the germ called sin, identifying it as the fallen nature received from Adam.[2]

Likewise, what was once a pristine "world," the Garden of Eden, has also been affected. The land, the animals, and the very air has been saturated by that one act. Be mindful that one chapter later, Genesis four, Adam and Eve became parents of two sons, Cain and Abel. By verse eight, Abel had been murdered. Murdered? Yes, murdered. And, the murderous spirit that prevailed in Cain was let loose in him, as well as in the atmosphere (for lack of stating it some other way). Pride, hate, selfishness, lies, immorality, sexism, idolatry, and the list goes on, are all the results of that single violation. Do I dare say that it proved to be not only detrimental, but deadly?

When George Lucas' blockbuster Star Wars movie franchise hit the big screen in 1977, one of the catch phrases was, "There's been an agitation in the force," meaning in simplistic language, that the good guys—the Jedi—had the ability or perception to sense the presence and/or plans of the bad guys—the Sith. When God's command was violated, God's presence and plans as represented by His creation were agitated. Of course, Jesus Christ has come to remove that agitation by His life, death, and resurrection, as the Apostle Paul poetically wrote to the Christians in Corinth: *"Death is swallowed up in victory...O death, where is thy sting? O grave, where is thy victory? The sting (or agitation) of death is sin; and the strength (or agitation) of sin is the law. But thanks be to God, which giveth us the victory through our Lord Jesus Christ"* (I Corinthians 15:54-57). However, outside of our conversion to Christ, the agitation remains. There's an agitation in the atmosphere.

It is important to appreciate the devastating effect that one single breach of God's law can have. Just as the tossed pebble in the lake creates ripples, and just like one pushed domino topples all of the rest, one lie leads to another. One "hit," arguably, leads to an addiction. Still further, the one lied on or the addict do not live in a bubble. Their lives come in contact with others, and the circle or line of involvement widens or lengthens, respectively. And, then, there is the societal impact. Families are disrupted, and likewise friendships. Often, law enforcement has to intervene, which leads to the involvement of the judicial system, and so on. However, of greater significance is the spiritual impact. God's law has been broken and a violation has occurred and has to be dealt with.

> "If, I had only known, I never would have gone (to the club). I'm so sorry." The words fell from the teenager's mouth with unbelievable regret. However, nothing he offered could bring back his friend who had been killed as a result of his drunk driving. People fail to heed God's warnings...They ignore the fact that they are responsible to God for their actions. A single sin—such as the sin of compromise—can lead to a number of other problems.[3]

When we have been plainly told, "don't," and we "do," that act and that sin ripple and domino, agitating God's created beings, and God's creation, in general. Whether we like it or not, or whether we believe it or not, there are consequences for our actions.

This, then, is why we, ourselves, feel victimized when we are violated. Someone or something has penetrated our space and invaded our proxemics. From rape to robbery, such intrusions are always unwelcomed and harmful. In fact, we almost never completely get over them, although we are taught by God's Word to forgive (St. Matthew 18:21-22). It is forgiving that helps in the healing process. To hold on to stuff only compounds the violation and holds us captive. "Some of us are so bound up in unforgiveness that we cannot get any further in life because the grudges we are holding prevent us from a breakthrough... Unforgiveness is wrong thinking. It makes you think you are holding someone else down but in actuality you are holding yourself down.[4] We must learn to move on with the help of God and time, and rest in God's Word, even as he said, *"Vengeance belongeth unto me, I will recompense (repay)...."* (Hebrews 10:30).

Dr. Charles E. Booth, pastor of the Mount Olivet Baptist Church, Columbus, Ohio, and mentor of mine, said, in a sermon, that Jesus never asked us to forgive and forget. He asks us to forgive, but our memory won't let us forget. He further states that when we have been wronged by someone, we are to forgive them, and even if we have moved on and twenty years have passed, when that person crosses our path, those initial feelings immediately return. We have forgiven, but we haven't forgotten. Such is the insult and the injury of the violation.

Note, also, the language of the Apostle Paul as he references his pain, having asked the Lord to remove it, no less than three times. He called it—whatever "it" was—*"a thorn in his flesh"* (II Corinthians 11:7). Bishop Rudolph McKissick, of the Full Gospel Baptist Fellowship and pastor of the Bethel Baptist Institutional Church, Jacksonville, Florida, stated in a sermon, that a thorn only has one purpose, which is to inflict pain. Something was tremendously agitating, disturbing, provoking, and hurting to the point that it made Paul terribly weak. He could only thank God for providing him with His sufficient grace that gave him the strength to endure.

Even the glorified Jesus still bears the wounds of the violations against His body. And, if anyone had the power to heal even their own wounds and forget, Jesus does. Granted, on the other side of His resurrection, those wounds are evidence of Who He is, and what He went through. In essence, from this perspective, they are medals of honor, even as He showed them as proof to his disciple, Thomas (St. John 20:27). However, those wounds, albeit healed wounds, are also kept as reminders of the inflicted pain, torture, and violation of His body, indicative of His ultimate sacrifice. We know that Jesus forgave His enemies, even from the cross (St. Luke 23:34), but the fact that He still bears the scars is indication that He has not forgotten, and neither should we.

To go against what we are told not to go against, then, leaves lasting problems and pain. It is as if a driver has ignored the law that one must come to a complete stop at a red light, before turning right on red. Or, one has come to a stop sign, but rather than stopping does a "rolling stop." How many accidents have been caused because of this kind of callous driving, when all would have been well if one simply came to a complete stop?

Still further think in terms of a barrier having been built in order to prevent passage through a dangerous cliff on the other side. The barrier is posted with a warning of no safe thru-way and proper detour signs point the safe way around. But some know-it-all traveler knows best. So, the traveler penetrates the barrier, violates the posted warning, and travels on his way, right to a fall. Now, that barrier could be advice indicating don't do it that way. It could be the no of a would-be companion that they are not ready and they need more time, or that they simply don't want to. Or, it could be that inner voice whispering or shouting, "you'd better not." Whatever the barrier may be, it is there for a reason. It is there for our protection, for the protection of others, and the protection of all who will be impacted by violating the barrier, including God's plan for our lives.

One day, while driving in the car, my youngest son, Timothy, who was about five or six years old, and just learning how to read, asked me the following question, as we'd come to a complete stop at a stop sign: "Daddy, how do you know when it's o.k. to go again, since the sign says 'stop'?" (Implicit in his curious and intuitive mind was, there was no "go" sign). My only response to him, almost without hesitation was, "We go when God says 'it's safe to go'." The reality is that no's are no's, even as stop signs are stops, and they must not be anything other than what they are until and unless God says otherwise.

When we are told what not to do, we should seek to take into account, as best we can, all of the ramifications that our willful decision will have if we choose to violate the same. Remember, being told "not to" is for the benefit of our being able to examine what lies behind the prohibition in order for us to appreciate what we are about to avoid—things like pain, addiction, disappointment, and failure. God leads us through seen and unseen dangers. Angels guide us and protect us in and out of various situations and circumstances. But, we must be responsible, aware, alert, and discerning for our own actions, as well, and learn to also appreciate the peace of where we are and what we have before we run the stop sign, bringing unforeseen agitation and disruption to the spiritual harmony previously enjoyed.

Chapter Six

Negativity and a Society Without Regrets

"You can't do wrong and get by," "look before you leap," and "you reap what you sow" are a few of the plethora of axioms that point to the fact that there are consequences to our actions, especially when our actions are harmful, detrimental, and sinful. I have mentioned the pain and punishments that are caused by violating God's Word that don't just affect the violator, but the violation also has impact on others and other circumstances. This chapter will seek to take a closer look then at where we find ourselves when we violate and don't respect God's law or any others.

In our country, various news agencies constantly publish reports about the backlogs in our court systems. For example, The News Tribune, in a 2007 article reported that the Pierce County Superior Court, in Denver, CO, had 2,460 unresolved criminal cases, of which 14% were older than 9 months. Justice delayed is justice denied.

Many communities don't have nearly enough law enforcement officers. In almost every major city police officers are overwhelmed and outnumbered. In my own state of Maryland, a state with a population of approximately 5.6 million, we have less than 15,000 full-time law enforcement officers.[1]

Our prison population had become for all intents and purposes a quasi society unto itself. Needless to say that our country's prison population has long since exceeded its maximum capacity. The U. S. Bureau of Justice Statistics (BJS) reports that one out of every 143 Americans is now in prison, with over 700 new inmates entering the system, weekly. This is staggering.

While crime and violence continue to escalate and spiral out of control, our nation's educational system is showing serious signs of failure. A study entitled, "The Economic Impact of the Achievement Gap in American Schools" by the consulting firm McKinsey was cited in the New York Times as stating, "In the 1950's and 1960's, the U. S. dominated the world in k-12 education...In the 1970's and 1980's, we still had a lead, albeit smaller...Today, we have fallen behind in both per capita high school graduates and their quality. Consequences to follow."[2] The study goes on to point out that in 2006, the Program for International Student Assessment measured the applied learning and problem-solving skills of 15 year-olds in 30 industrialized countries ranked the U. S. as 25th out of 30 in math and 24th in science.

Meanwhile, according to the American Religious Identification Survey, the percentage of self-identified Christians has fallen 10 percentage points since 1990, from 86 to 76 percent...Meanwhile the number of people willing to describe themselves as atheists or agnostics has increased about fourfold from 1990 to 2009, from 1 million to about 3.6 million.[3] While we are experiencing an increase in criminal behavior, our nation's Christian faith is diminishing.

Newsweek writer, Jon Meacham, states, "While we remain a nation decisively shaped by religious faith, our politics and our culture are, in the main, less influenced by movements and arguments of an explicitly Christian character than they were even five years ago...The proportion of Americans who think religion "can answer all or most of today's problems" is now at a historic low 48 percent.[4]

Illegalities, criminal behavior, and immoral living have all but become common place. There is more wrong at work in our nation than we literally know what to do with. From the previously mentioned effort of the War on Drugs, to task forces established to deal with gangs and gang violence, to white collar crime, to domestic abuse, to petty theft, all the way to corporate ponzi schemes, there is no doubt that we have more than enough that's gone wrong. The questions are: where is the guilt? and where is the regret? I have alluded to the notion that, generally, our sense of guilt has become passé. "Crime doesn't pay," (another axiom that can be added to the aforementioned) may imply that criminals will be caught, persecuted, and punished, but what is the general response of the criminal, or even any of us, who does wrong? Are we genuinely remorseful and repentant regarding what we have done? Or, have we conceded that God's prohibitions no longer are relevant, that societal laws are made to be broken, and we are empowered to determine our own rules, ethics, and morals because anarchy, in its broadest sense, which is to say the absence of principles and standards beyond the political world, already exists? Indeed, for many, it would seem that crime *does* pay.

Granted, so much certainly seems out of control and out of order, indicative of times predicted for the eschaton. If nothing else, we seem to have exceeded pre-flood days, Sodom and Gomorrah days, and other biblical and post-biblical days of debauchery, violence, and sinfulness.

Once lines have been crossed and barriers have been breached, as another saying goes "it's hard to put the genie back into the bottle." Child psychologists warn parents to hold firm their no's, because if you give the child an inch, the child will take two, and, children grow up. Adults will take a step, and if they think they've gotten away with it, they'll take two more. In Greek mythology, the gods made the first woman without human parents and gave her unique gifts. Her name was Pandora. She carried around a large jar—which we've come to refer to as "Pandora's box." It contained all kinds of evils to be unleashed on humanity, if opened. Indeed, she was warned by Zeus to keep it closed. However, one of the gifts she'd been given was curiosity. It eventually got the best of her, and she opened the jar, unleashing all kinds of evil upon the human race which seemingly had no way of being put back. Such would seem to be our present plight, and save for the return of Jesus, is it too late to reclaim some semblance of social, moral, ethical, and spiritual sanity? If nothing else, a case is certainly being made for us to sure up whatever boundaries remain, as well as continue to affirm the scriptures, because we don't have much left that hasn't already been crossed or let loose. When we witness the actions and attitudes of so many of our children, who have been wrongfully influenced and seduced into thinking that a life of gang-banging, pimping, hustling and cursing is normal behavior, we have to conclude that we're in serious trouble.

As bad as our condition is, there is a sense, if not a belief, that God has placed in the soul of the universe a certain balance that brings adjustments in His favor, given that this is a moral universe. All of the police, judges, parents, and even preachers in the world may not be able to right all of the wrongs, but there is another power.

The Book of Numbers records the statement: *"… and be sure your sins will find you out"* (32:23). In First Corinthians, albeit in the context of judgment, can be found this statement: *"Therefore judge nothing before the time, until the Lord come, who will bring to light the hidden things of darkness…"* (4:5). This is why we say that what's done in the dark will come to the light. Again, I assert that there is a system of checks and balances that is operative and controlled by God.

We have become accustomed to hearing it said with regards to our own guilt or remorse, as well as others, that the only reason we're sorry is because we broke the so-called eleventh commandment: "Thou shalt not get caught." The implication is that as long as the misdeed or sin had occurred or was occurring that there was no guilt felt or associated with the behavior. I contend that, to some degree, guilt kicks in not necessarily during or after, but it is a part of the decision to be disobedient, even from the beginning. It is guilt that makes us hide our tracks, disguise ourselves, and it is a part of the process. As I have mentioned, there is little doubt but that we have blurred the distinctions between right and wrong, but I will not totally concede to any conclusion that ultimately the human race does not know right from wrong, and therefore has been able to turn off its sense of shame, as Dr. Taylor previously alluded to. It has been said that no one is above the law. It must also be said that, with the exception of socio-paths and reprobates, that no one is without some measure of guilt. It is guilt that initially causes us to think twice, even if for a second, and then stays with us, perhaps even becoming more profound over time, even if we believe we've gotten away with something. Some are able to compartmentalize it, but that does not remove it. It's always there.

The word that should more likely be associated with getting caught is regret. If we are to wave any flag concerning the violation of laws, standards, and boundaries, as a society, we may want to give attention to how punishments: sentencings, convictions, remunerations, and probations impact regret. I assert that it is regret that occurs when we're caught or found out, and in order to avoid iniquities (knowingly repeating the same act of sin) or recidivism, a more challenging way of increasing regret needs to be given attention; that is, if the purpose is to work with the violator in order to keep the violator from doing it again. Still further, one cannot be made to feel guilty. Guilt, I believe, must come from an inner corrective. Just ask David and refer to his 51st Psalm. On the other hand, even if one does not demonstrate regret for one's actions, or for having been caught, one can still be made to feel or experience regret based on the response and penalty (penalties) given. By and large, we have developed a society that has been made to feel no regret, because it fears none.

I admit that I have painted a rather dismal picture of our present landscape, but what else should we expect when we violate God's laws, as well as our own civil and moral laws? Disobedience is destructive. However, I hasten to add that all is not lost.

Remember, God has placed in the soul of the universe a certain balance. There does exist the destructiveness that disobedience brings; and here we are primarily referring (but not exclusively) to the adherence of not doing what God asks us not to do. Living according to God's Word and being obedient to His prohibitions are the basic underpinnings that help maintain whatever civility that remains. Look at it from this perspective. What kind of society would presently exist if there was no Church, or if God's people didn't make the difference in communities, schools, corporations, military services, politics, and governments, perhaps even tipping the scale?

In spite of all that's gone and is going wrong, there are strong Christian families, there are countless young people who do the right thing by saying, "no" to the wrong thing, and there are those of us who having done wrong and been caught, have experienced regret and have re-established the boundary, and have been given another chance. After all the evils were let loose out of Pandora's box, at the very bottom there was found one last thing to emerge, and that was hope.

PART TWO
NEGATIVITY:
SPIRITUAL

"But as it is written, Eye hath not seen nor ear heard, neither have entered into the heart of man, the things which God hath prepared for them that love him."

-I Corinthians 2:9

CHAPTER SEVEN

NEGATIVITY AND DISLIKING WHAT GOD DISLIKES

If we were to create a collage of snapshots highlighting our nation's historic events that have occurred over the past one hundred years, the end result would tell the story of something quite unique and remarkable. The majority of almost every significant event can be traced to some aspect of rebellion or resistance; it was the dislike of some system, treatment, war, disease, or law that led to a reaction against said issue.

It was at a time, respective to what was going on, that some form of dislike began to develop and became personified in the lives of usually a few persons who rose up to speak the proverbial "truth to power" and declare, "This must end. This will not be tolerated. This must change. This is wrong." It was the dislike, and in many instances, the disdain, of issues that gave rise to peace treaties, civil rights (desegregation), voter registration laws, medical and technological advances, and social reforms.

Without a doubt, such a collage would not just tell the story of our nation's past one hundred years, but a similar collage of world history, in general, would be replete with successes and victories that were precipitated by protests, battles, picket lines, boycotts, and whistle blowers. To be sure, it takes courage to "stand up against," or to "speak out about." Yet, time after time someone has individually mustered the will or galvanized a group for the purpose of demonstration. Why? Because the sense was that some things aren't right, they cannot be tolerated, and they must not be put up with.

Now, that we are in the dawning years of this 21st century, there seems to be in the realm of sensibility a certain nostalgia that longs for the passion of past courage that gave rise to challenge the powers-that-be. We have become so accommodating, tolerant, and accepting. We have practically been conditioned to like everything. And, if we don't, in the name of tolerance, we are constrained to hold our peace. Weren't we better children? Weren't we a better people and society when we had firmer and stronger underpinnings with regards to what we did not like, especially when it lined up with the dislikes of God's will, as found in His Word?

An understanding and appreciation of God's dislikes and prohibitions help us to gain clarity and guide us in knowing precisely where God does not want us to go and exactly what God does not want us to do. There are things that God does not like. We have previously touched on God's sovereignty. Let us also touch on God's holiness. Interestingly, one of the best descriptions of God's holiness is found in negative form.

There is none holy as the Lord: for there is none beside thee: neither is there any rock like our God.

First Samuel 2:2 explains that He is most "holy" and that no one is as holy as He is.[1] The familiar praise and worship song, "There Is None Like Him," has its roots in this verse. Although the Hebrew word for holy, *qados,* essentially means separate or apart, such is not to be understood as an attribute of God, but the very foundation of His being. The prophet Isaiah wrote that seraphims cried out to each other, *"Holy, holy, holy, is the Lord of hosts..."* (6:3a)

To say that God is holy, is to describe God as pure. In recognizing the purity of God, we are practically forced to do so using negative language. Since the word pure is an absolute, it can best be defined by what it isn't or lacks. Pure connotes homogenous, perfection, chaste, and clean. But when we read that pure is "not mixed, free from impurities or adulterants, containing nothing inappropriate or unnecessary, without faults, and free from discordant qualities,"[2] our understanding is much clearer and sharper, and it is based on what pure is not.

It is the basis of the holiness of God as being understood as pure that the traditional and aforementioned understanding of "separate" is only a derived meaning, and not the primary. (The likelihood is that the idea of separate or separated has more to do with God's expectation[s] of us, anyway, as found in II Corinthians 6:17.)[3] It is, therefore, the purity of God which makes God holy, that makes anything unholy abhorrent to Him. Yes, we know that God is love and that God loves (I John 4:8; St. John 3:16), but God is spoken of as hating evil and sin (Psalm 53:5; 97:10; 119:128; Hebrews 1:9a). Moreover, God himself took the time to specify those things He considers as such, so that there won't be any confusion.

I recently read an insight about what God hates that challenged my theology (unfortunately, I'm unable to document the source). I read that God (or Jesus) never asked us to love all, or everything/everyone. Jesus said, *"But I say unto you, love your enemies..."* (St. Matthew 5:44a). God has enemies that will forever remain enemies. We are to love our enemies, but we don't have to love the enemies of God...starting with Satan.

Whatever Satan, who is the author of confusion, deceit, and sin, imitates or tries to orchestrate is therefore an affront to God. God has limits, standards, and boundaries, and His love is such that He wants there to be no ambiguity regarding what He wants and what He does not want. There is good and there is evil. There is right and there is wrong.

Unfortunately, we as God's created beings have sought to "dumb down" and compromise God's limits, standards, and boundaries. We know what God does not want, but we have devised our own limits, standards, and boundaries. One aspect of this has become so pervasive that theologians have even given it a name: situation ethics. Situation ethics, from a Christian point of view, is a protest against flexible Christian legalism (God's law/Word) as it should apply to all Christians. Therefore, it seeks to change or adjust said law(s) to fit the time or situation.

Waldo Beach, in his book entitled, *Christian Ethics in the Protestant Tradition*, concludes that situation ethics proved in time to slide down a slippery slope towards the ethics of improvisation and become normless.[4] The father of this ethic was an Episcopal priest named Joseph Fletcher. He was attempting to find a middle way between God's law and "libertinism (which said that there were no moral absolutes, meaning that each individual was to follow his or her own conscience and that what really mattered were outcomes)."[5] Fletcher was suggesting that God's law did not take into account the many and varied circumstances and decisions. As a result he proposed that given the human factor of maintaining God's law that we could still do right by asking ourselves, What is the loving thing to do (based on St. John 13:34-35)? The problem I have is, in and of ourselves, we don't always know what the loving thing to do is. Fortunately, we have God's Word, especially as exemplified by Jesus, to help and show us how to respond and react in situations.

God does not need us to adjust or redefine His Word. We may not like it, and we may find it difficult, but our attitude towards it will not change its efficacy. If nothing else, when it's all said and done, we know what God expects from us, and we know what He does not expect from us. Furthermore, and more to the point, is that we are to see ourselves as not only agreeing with God, but being able to be His proponents and spokespersons. We are to stand up for the very things that God affirms. If God has an issue with something, so should we. If God doesn't agree with something, nor should we. And, when we witness an offense to God's Word, we are to do whatever possible to set it right. Inasmuch as our focus is on the negativity of God's Word, Harrelson writes: "(God's Word) gives us ground for cries of protest and outrage, even when we may not know exactly what we ought positively to recommend,"[6] we certainly have no excuse knowing what he does not want us to stand for and/or do.

CHAPTER EIGHT

NEGATIVITY AND DOING WITHOUT

One of the ironies of life is how we come to truly appreciate the blessings of people and things in life. For example, some have learned to appreciate having money, because they know what it's really like to have been broke. Others appreciate good health, because they've experienced sickness and hospitalization. The likelihood is that all of us can appreciate the sunshine, because there has been a time, or two, when we've been caught in a storm. Consequently, it would seem that, again, we learn to appreciate, or we discover the value of people and things having experienced their opposite.

There is also another way that we learn to appreciate and value the blessings of life, especially when we are open to God's will in our lives. There is much to be said in or by adapting a divesting attitude. (I am going to approach this from an attitudinal point of view. However, the lesson or lessons learned can equally be experienced when or if we find ourselves literally without.)

I recently preached a message entitled, "The Teacher of Affliction," based on Isaiah 30:20. A part of my proposition was that spiritual maturity usually doesn't occur during the "ups" in our lives. Spiritual maturity is more likely to occur during the "downs" in our lives. The Apostle Paul wrote in II Corinthians 12:9b-10 these strange words that can only be appreciated by those who truly understand how negatives impact us, from a godly perspective:

> *Most gladly therefore will I rather glory in my infirmities, that the power of Christ may rest upon me.*

> *Therefore I take pleasure in infirmities, in reproaches, in necessities, in persecutions, in distresses for Christ's sake: for when I am weak, then am I strong.*

The Apostle Paul nowhere refers to having come to his state of maturity because of having experienced deliverances and healings. To the contrary, he credited his difficulties. The reality was, Paul still had a thorn problem (12:7) that he apparently never got rid of, nor did God take away, even after he prayed for its removal three times, as we've previously mentioned. Yet, at the same time, he testified about having heard from the Lord, how his strength was developed in his weakness, how he received sufficient grace, how he would rather glory in his downs, and how he had learned to take pleasure in his downs, as well – astonishing conclusions and resolves, especially after realizing that they are the results of not having been delivered from his predicament. His learning and maturity took place in the context of one extreme; having experienced one extreme and then its opposite.

This concept may seem unusual, but it's not new. Over and over, Jesus taught about divesting, in one way or another. In other words, the extreme down doesn't necessarily have to be painful. It can simply be the experience of being down and without. Therefore, Jesus taught about being poor in spirit, hungering and thirsting after righteousness, self-denial, and forsaking mother, father, sisters, brothers, houses, and land. He instructed his disciples, saying, *"Take nothing for your journey, neither staves, nor scrip, neither bread, neither money; neither have two coats a piece"* (St. Luke 9:3). Jesus, Himself practiced what He preached (taught) based on His self-disclosure about His lack of permanent lodging, *"Foxes have holes, and birds of the air have nests; but the Son of man hath not where to lay his head"* (St. Luke 9:58).

It is in the living without or in the not having that spiritual growth and maturity takes place. Our mothers and fathers in slavery are a tremendous paradigm of this reality. Having been raped and robbed in practically every way, they developed unmistakable prayer language, freedom songs, and a defiant faith. Parenthetically, with all that this present generation has in the way of opportunities, advancements and possessions, what evidences of spiritual maturity can we show, let alone leave for succeeding generations? There is truth in the saying, "With more we have less, and with less we had more."

Since the beginning of the year, I've been teaching our Deacons Ministry's Saturday Church School Bible Class using a book entitled, *Seeing Through the Eyes of Jesus*, by John F. Baggett. The most recent chapter discussed focused on "Jesus and the Destitute." One of the points in this particular chapter has to deal with The Advantage of Having Nothing. Baggett makes the case that not only are the destitute the object of Jesus' affinity, but it is precisely the fact that they don't have that positions them for Jesus' compassion, as well as gives them an advantage over those of the opposite extreme; namely, the wealthy. Baggett writes, "In this world, the rich hold an overwhelming advantage over the destitute. In the realm of God, the world of the Spirit, the destitute hold an overwhelming advantage over the rich."[1]

Such an advantage is based on the idea that the absence of things free us from prioritizing on and trusting what we have and amplifies our need. Need is one of the foremost prerequisites and indicators that opens us up to a relationship with God. Simply put, those whose needs are "met" have no need for God.

The rich, young ruler (St. Luke 18:18-23) went away very sad, for he preferred his treasures on earth, as opposed to treasures in Heaven. He wanted eternal life, but he refused to have an eternal relationship with the Lord. He never realized how needy he really was.

When we discover that Jesus is the only true source of satisfaction when it comes to meeting our need(s), we find ourselves relying on Him, as we grow in our love and affection for Him. In the best sense of the word, our need leads us to dependency. There's an old hymn that states, *"I'd rather have Jesus than silver or gold..."*

Dependency, in this vein, is a good thing, for when we are down due to some adversity or just trying to make ends meet, the best support and help is Jesus.

I've generally believed, since going into ministry, that most people who join the church on Sunday mornings haven't necessarily been convicted during the highs of that respective service. I contend that usually it was something that occurred during the days leading up to that Sunday—some crisis, affliction, adversity, or difficulty—that forced them to know that they had a need, and that they'd better get to some church and publicly profess what they've already professed privately – that they needed and had accepted Jesus. The point is that more often than not, our negative experiences and circumstances are fertile ground for our spiritual growth, because Jesus Who came down through forty-two generations meets us where we are, whether we were "sinking deep in sin," or in the midst of "many dangers, toils, and snares."

Dr. Gardner C. Taylor told a story once about preaching during a revival service many years ago, in a rural Virginia church, one evening, when a storm came up. He said that right in the middle of his sermon there was a loud clap of thunder, followed by lightening, and then all the electricity in that little, wooden church went out. He paused for a moment, as immediate darkness filled the sanctuary. "Then," he said, "I heard a voice of a brother coming from the rear. The brother yelled, 'keep preachin' preacher. We can still see Jesus in the dark.'"

CHAPTER NINE

NEGATIVITY AND UNANSWERED PRAYER

One of the great questions of the ages is, Why does God say no? This question usually is asked in the context of what we consider to be unanswered prayer. Thus, the question more frequently asked is, Why doesn't God answer some prayers? Now, we can be pontifical and pious by responding that it's God's prerogative, because He is God, and it's really not ours to question. God is sovereign, and can do whatever He wants to. Such is true, but when God says no and when God commands us not to do something He's just exercising His sovereignty, He's implementing His will for our lives. Ours is to seek to get a handle on His will.

I would be the first to admit that I would always want God to say yes. The reality is, although we may not always say so, do we really want a "yes-God?" C'mon, isn't that part of a God's job description? Don't we want a genie in a bottle kind of God Who offers us three wishes? (And, for the sake or argument, my first wish would be to have unlimited wishes.) Don't we want a Santa Claus kind of God, or "a cosmic bell-hop" kind of God, as Dr. Jeremiah Wright, retired pastor of the Trinity U.C.C. Church, Chicago, Illinois, said in a sermon? A God, especially a good God, should always want to please, come through, and bless. What's up with all of these no's, don'ts, and "thou shalt nots?" "Why shouldn't I be healed? Why can't I get that job? Why won't you bring my child back home? I was a good parent."

Inasmuch as we believe that the God of the Bible is God "all by Himself," meaning that He is I AM, Yahweh, Creator, and Savior, among countless other descriptions, characteristics, attributes, and names, it also means that all other gods are false, or at best idols. It is this totally comprehensive and all inclusive God, then, Who, as exemplified in the Scriptures, has an interest in us. God created us. God knows us. God loves us. God saved us. Therefore, whatever no's, boundaries, stop signs, and "thou shalt nots," He gives must be seen in light of His blessings and favor for us and not always as punitive and flat-out denials.

We must be mindful, as well as grateful, that God's interest in us is so uniquely wonderful that God's Son, Jesus Christ, invites us to experience the same kind of relationship that He has: a parent-child relationship. We can call God, "Our Father" (St. Matthew 6:9).

A father provides and a father protects. A father also disciplines. A part of being a good disciplinarian isn't just being one to punish or chastise, but knowing when to simply say no. And, most parents—fathers or mothers—say no not because they're mean or don't want to be bothered, but because their experience, as opposed to the child's, allows them the benefit of seeing, if not knowing, the big picture. Their refusals are for the child's best interest. It's all about love. Without a doubt, then, our Heavenly Father always sees and knows what we can't see and don't know. Ours is to be appreciative of God's prohibitions and denials, even though we wonder why, want to pout, and are often disappointed.

This subject of why God says no is so compelling that practically an entire cottage industry has emerged. Conferences, counselors, sermons, and books are plentiful. Indeed, a theology has developed, seeking to explain and justify this negative aspect of God's will. However, I have come to learn and appreciate that the Bible is the best commentary of itself. Therefore, let's cite some of the reasons the Scriptures give in response to God's no's.

> As much as we may not like it, God's no can be punishment. In the Book of Numbers, Moses was told by God that because he did not believe Him or trust Him enough in the eyes of Israel that he would not be allowed to enter into the Promised Land (20:12).

> When we have undisclosed sin (iniquity), it stymies and can block our prayer life. Psalm 66:18 states, *"If I regard iniquity in my heart, the Lord will not hear me..."*

The Book of James, chapter 4, tells us that we ask but don't receive because we *"ask amiss, that we may consume it for our lusts"* (v. 3). In a similar vein, we may have asked without faith, or we didn't ask in His (Jesus') name. Alice Cullinam wrote in an article, "Why God Sometimes Says 'No,'" that perhaps our trust during times of unanswered prayer and God's no answers are good indicators of the depth or the shallowness of our faith.[1] *"Lord, I believe; help thou mine unbelief"* (St. Mark 9:24).

God says no in order for us to avoid temptation. We may desire to travel somewhere or to participate in something (like my high school classmates' party), but such an open door could potentially put us in a compromising position that would best be avoided by not going, at all. Otherwise, if allowed, the temptation could be seen as a test (I Corinthians 10:13).

Paul, like so many, did not get the answer he wanted regarding the removal of his "thorn," but he did get an answer. And, the answer he received opened up an entirely new revelation and appreciation from and of God. God's no's take us into dimensions we would otherwise miss; dimensions that grow us through God's grace and strengthens us, even in our weakness (II Corinthians 12:7-10).

God has His own reason(s) that we aren't privy to. Deuteronomy 29:29a states, *"The secret things belong unto the Lord our God..."* Also, note Isaiah 55:8 and 9.

God says no, because He has something better for us. During my first pastorate in Reading, Pennsylvania, my wife, Monique, and I were house shopping. At the time, we were living in a townhouse. Our shopping led us to what we believed would be our home. When we saw it, without ever going inside, we sat in our car and prayed for it to be ours. This was, also, during the height of the so-called "name it and claim it" movement during the eighties. Needless to say, we were outbid and did not get that house.

Not long after, out of nowhere, I received a call at our townhouse from someone identifying himself as a realtor representing a new development. He asked if I would be interested in seeing the parcels of land available for new construction. When we met at the development site I could not have been any less impressed by this soft spoken, underconfident person. He almost seemed like he wasn't there. One thing led to another. My wife and I agreed on an excellent parcel, which we got for free, pending that we would build on that site. (Yes, I did wonder what was underneath, in the ground.) Nevertheless, a contractor was hired, and we were in a brand new home, at less than what it would have cost us for the other and older home. We only lived in that home for three years when I accepted a call to pastor in Petersburg, Virginia. Having hardly any equity was no problem for God. At the time of our departure, the city of Reading was experiencing growth in the insurance industry and businesses were hiring and relocating people from all over. We sold our home at a price that would amount to a 30% appreciation. When we moved to Petersburg, we were able to take our time and get essentially the kind of home we really wanted. But wait. There's more.

After we had the home built in Reading and had moved in, I wanted to send the realtor a basket to thank him. My dealing with him had been either by phone (he would call me, or I would call an extension at his business number) or in person. I was aware of the real estate agency that he worked for, which was a reputable agency. When I called the agency and pressed the numbers for his extension I was unable to get him, nor was there a voicemail for him, anymore. I, subsequently, called the agency in order to speak with anyone, because all I needed was the address. The person on the other end told me that they had never heard of the person who I asked for, let alone had never worked for their agency. I concluded that our prospect for a Dale Carnegie scholarship had simply vanished, and that we'd been entertaining an angel, unaware.

Finally, Mary and Martha help us understand that His no's are often for some Greater Glory. These sisters sent word to Jesus on the behalf of their sick brother, who was also Jesus' friend, that he was about to die. Jesus refused to come to help his sick friend. Even worse, when Lazarus died, Jesus continued where He was for two more days. Jesus' refusal to come when they wanted Him to come, gave rise for the raising of Lazarus from the dead. St. John 11:4 states: *"This sickness is not unto death, but for the glory of God, that the Son of God might be glorified thereby."*

It could be that what we consider to be unanswered prayer of God's no's in response to our prayers has more to do with God's will being done. The aforementioned biblical reasons are just some of the ways that can help us put into context this very thought. We're looking for answers (usually answers that fit our expectations and desires. God is looking to carry out His will. Keep in mind that the fourth emphasis in the "Model Prayer" that Jesus taught His disciples was to pray, *"Thy will be done on earth as it is in heaven."* (St. Matthew 6:10b). What we have to learn and accept is that God's will won't prevail in our respective lives until our own will is curtailed. Yet, most of our prayers prioritize our will without hardly any petitioning for God's.

When I was a senior in college, I wanted my last year as a member of the tennis team to be my best. I wanted to end my collegiate tennis career in a blaze of glory being the first player since the coach, Coach Tom, eight years earlier, to be undefeated. Eastern College was, at that time, a relatively small Christian college of about 1,300 students. For the most part, but not exclusively, we played other Christian schools. In addition to our team prayer, prior to each match, I would pray privately myself, "Lord, let me be victorious over my opponent." After the first of thirteen matches that senior season, I had won the first three and was well on my way towards my goal. Prior to the fourth match, just after my warm ups, I prayed my prayer. When the match was over that afternoon, I discovered during the after-match perfunctory handshaking with the other team that my opponent had prayed a similar prayer. Needless to say, he had won, and I ended up being 12 and 1 for the season and still brought home the MVP trophy for that year. But, I learned a meaningful lesson: God was not interested in my ego tripping...in my will, regardless of how mundane or unimportant in the bigger scheme of life's issues. When I should have simply been playing to glorify Him, first, I desired to seek to glorify myself, and God said, "no."

CHAPTER TEN

NEGATIVITY AND THE FIRST PSALM

The first Psalm in the Hebrew hymnal opens with what it means to be happy or blessed by not doing certain things. In a manner of speaking, the message of this psalm teaches that happiness is best attained and appreciated when we recognize the judgment, consequences, and punishment we could have received have been avoided, because we did not participate, we did not indulge, and we did not act.

One of the best feelings, and one of the best happy moments, is when we know that we could have done, gone, said, and so on, but we didn't, even though and unfortunately, others did. And the others subsequently had to "pay a price," but we didn't, because...we didn't.

Once again, we are called upon to consider the teaching that uses language that is negative in order to instruct and avoid circumstances that are outside of God's will and desire for us. The unique aspect of the opening three lines of the first verse of the first Psalm, however, is the fact that reward is attached to the negative prohibition. The Psalm teaches what we are not to do, and then it promises (by implication) that if we don't do these things we will be happy...we will be blessed. In fact, the promise of happiness borders on the superlative, inasmuch as the Hebrew language is transliterated as "How happy!" or "Oh, the happiness!" Obviously, those who do engage in doing the prohibitions won't be happy; not even close. The psalm states that they "are not so," (vs. 4a). Eugene Peterson says that such persons are like "windblown dust."[1]

Ironically, the same negative language that is used at the beginning of the Psalm to give instruction and reward to those who would adhere uses negative language towards the end of the Psalm to indicate the fate of those who did not adhere. *"Therefore the ungodly shall not stand in the judgment, nor sinners in the congregation of the righteous"* (vs. 5). The psalm begins with those who would be blessed or happy, and it ends with those who would be cursed.

I have never completely bought in to the common understanding that happiness is relative or conditional. I understand the argument that there are certain things and certain moments that make us happy, if not happier, but that argument is based on a secular understanding of happiness. Granted, the opening verse of the psalm teaches that happiness is still conditional, but unlike the secular understanding that happiness comes and goes based on moments and events, this psalm asserts that happiness can be sustained; that one can live happily, lightheartedly, enthusiastically, and joyfully, without having to wait to celebrate a birthday or receive a raise.

Modern psychology tells us to emphasize the positive; God begins by emphasizing the negative. The happy,

happy man is marked by the things he does not do, the places to which he does not go, by the books he does not read, by the movies he does not watch, by the company he does not keep. Surely that's a strange way to begin!

God begins this book (of psalms/hymns) not with the power of positive thinking, but with the power of negative thinking![2]

The case is made that the person who would be a happy person begins by avoiding certain things in life; things that make happiness impossible to occur because they are detrimental, ruinous, and... ungodly. Therefore, the psalm states, *"Oh the happiness of the person who walks not in the counsel of the ungodly..."* Probably, one of the things that leads most of us astray is when we listen to the wrong voice, or voices. More of us have found ourselves in trouble because we paid attention to the wrong source, only to eventually find ourselves asking ourselves, "Why did I ever listen to him?" or "Why did I ever listen to her?" The wrong words that come from the world can only lead to sorrow and pain. Therefore, the psalmist's first wise words are, "Whatever you do, if you want to have a sure 'nuf happy life, don't listen to people who don't mean you any good," (author's paraphrase). The Living Bible paraphrases, *"Oh, the joys of those who do not follow evil men's advice..."* In other words, if we want to be happy, heed the advice: "Don't Listen to Everybody."

Then, the psalmist states that happiness is found by *"standing not in the way of sinners."* This does not mean that we should have absolutely no dealings with those who are sinners. Remember, Jesus prayed in St. John 17 that we would remain in the world;

just not of the world (vss.11-16). Furthermore, Jesus was rightfully accused of being a friend of sinners (St. Matthew 11:19). However, His aim was never to join them in their sinful state; but rather to lead them into having them join Him in a higher state. This part of the verse admonishes we are not to stand in the way of sinners, meaning that we are not to participate in their sinful activities. If we are to be happy, we must heed the further advice, not to hang out with those who mean us no good.

The last part of this verse instructs that in order to be happy, in order to be blessed, "do not sit in the seat of the scornful." The ungodly person has his/her "counsel," the sinner has his/her "way," and the scornful has his/her "seat". The implication is that of a professor's chair. The happy person avoids being in the classroom with a professor whose only instructions are anti-God lectures. "Note the progression in wickedness—the ungodly, the sinner, the scornful; and the corresponding progression in backsliding—walking, standing, sitting. As the company gets worse sin increases its hold."[3]

In this one, single verse we discover that Godly happiness is attained and maintained when we know what not to do. We are to stay away from the paths and places walked and used by those who have no love for God or His law. When we avoid such influences, we cannot help but find delight in God and his law, as well as want to enjoy such all day; hence, we will be oh, so happy. It's not that we're missing out on anything (that the world has to offer). The fact is, we're gaining much, much more.

Happiness, then, is really appreciating the peace and the joy of not being in trouble. It's appreciating not running with the wrong crowd. It's appreciating not or no longer being an addict. It's appreciating not being in prison. It's knowing that we could but we aren't. It's knowing *"there but for the grace of God..."* So, the psalmist begins the hymnal rejoicing in the prospect of real happiness; stay in God's law and stay out of trouble.

Macleans is a Canadian periodical that my father has been reading for years, somewhat akin to our *Times*. Recently, he gave me a copy of it, and asked me to read an article featuring an interview with an 86 year old monk who has been living in Canadian monasteries for the past seven decades, named Brother Gaston Deschamps. Among other things, he discussed silence, modern life "follies," and his few visits out into the modern world; his first visit outside of the monastery, having joined in 1941, was in 1956, some 15 years later. And, the truth-of-the-matter is, he has had no desire to leave. Only health necessities have forced him to do so.

What caught my attention was his last quote in the interview that had to do with his present state of being. He fully recognized that having been sequestered for almost all of his life that much of the world had passed him by, but he had found his calling, void of worldly trappings, noise, and violence. He indicated that he has had little interest in radio or television, but newspapers have been available. He is also aware, in his words, that we (the outside world) have removed God from every aspect of life. "When you lose faith in God, you lose faith in life...We've become too preoccupied with what is on the outside. I can't say it any other way. You have to live on the inside. It's good for the spirit..." All of that, and more, brought him to conclude with the following statement regarding his own happiness:

Next Sunday I'm going to receive the Sacrament of the Sick, which is what is given to the gravely ill and the dying. I've been condemned to death. I had a heart attack in 1998, and I've had bouts of angina since then. The veins to my heart are almost completely blocked. I've had treatment, but the doctors have said that they can't do anything more because more treatment would kill me. So, I'm just waiting quietly for death to take me. And I'm happy, because I know how I've lived and where I'm going.[4]

It is the Bible commentarian John Phillips who wrote, "The devil has no happy old men."[5]

CHAPTER ELEVEN

NEGATIVITY AND THE UNPARDONABLE SIN

One of the most significant reasons why we need and desire to have a relationship with God, through His Son, Jesus Christ, is because we believe that in spite of our sins, God "looked beyond our faults and saw our needs." He saw our needs to be loved, to be redeemed, and to be forgiven. God accepts us, when we accept Jesus, and gives us a brand new beginning, regardless of our past (2 Corinthians 5:17). Who wouldn't want to serve a God like that? We love Him, because He first loved us, and even when we do wrong having been saved, as long as we're sincere in our repentance of His unconditional love, He still forgives us (I John 1:9).

Knowing that God is a forgiving God, then what is this declaration given by His Son, Jesus, that has come to be known as "the unpardonable sin?"

Wherefore I say unto you, All manner of sin and blasphemy shall be forgiven unto men: but the blasphemy against the Holy Ghost shall not be forgiven unto men. (St. Matthew 12:31).

If ever there was a giant negative, this would be it. We find no wiggle room, no hint of grace, not even a chance to explain. Here we come to an absolute, "NO WAY!" Jesus states that whatever else you don't do, make sure that you include this on the top of the do not do list, because if you violate this warning and blaspheme against the Holy Spirit, there is absolutely no forgiveness. "To blaspheme is to slander someone. In the Bible, to blaspheme was to insult or demean the person, name, or character of God. Rather than honoring God, a person guilty of blasphemy cursed or reviled God and His name through derogatory words or actions."[1]

There are two significant verses that set the tone for understanding these words of Jesus: St. John 3:18 and 36:

He that believeth on him is not condemned: but he that believeth not is condemned already, because he hath not believed in the name of the only begotten Son of God.

And

He that believeth on the Son hath everlasting life: and he that believeth not the Son shall not see life; but the wrath of God abideth on him.

Based on these two verses, having no belief in Jesus as God's Son and one's Savior and/or to reject Jesus as being such is the ultimate sin. Consequently, to not believe in Jesus, Who He is, and/or to reject Him leads to one's condemnation. "The true unforgivable sin is permanently rejecting Jesus. Thus, speaking against the Holy Spirit is equivalent to rejecting Christ with such finality that no future repentance is possible."[2] Why? Because, as the Apostle Paul wrote to the Corinthian Christians, that the Holy Spirit was received by them that they would know the things that God had freely given that is salvation (I Corinthians 2:12-14). "The Holy Spirit persuades us to accept Jesus and all the blessings he brings, but if we refuse to submit to the Holy Spirit, preferring to call good evil and evil good, how can the Gospel avail to him? The deliberate refusal of the grace of God is one sin which by its very nature is irremediable."[3]

The context of Jesus' words grew out of a horrible accusation that was leveled against Him by the Pharisees, one of Judaism's religious leadership parties, who rejected Jesus as being Messiah. In St. Matthew 12:24-30, the Pharisees had witnessed the miraculous healing and delivering power of Jesus upon those in need. Rather than affirming what they'd seen and giving God the praise for it, they chose to blaspheme or slander Jesus by calling him Beelzebub, an Old Testament pagan deity (II Kings 1:2) and a demon in league with the devil, thereby, crediting the work of Jesus to the evil work of the devil.

Amazingly, in Jesus' response, He goes as far as stating that anyone who would say a blasphemous word against Him would still be forgiven.

> Speaking (or acting) out against Jesus and His ministry is subject to forgiveness because such words or acts of rejection come from misunderstanding the reality of his person and work. However, once the Holy Spirit works in people's lives, convicting and convincing them of the truth of the Gospel (St. John 16:8-11) or correcting

misunderstandings about Jesus, a subsequent persistent and decisive rejecting of the Holy Spirit's work regarding Jesus results in permanent judgment. Persistent obstinacy leads to permanent condemnation.[4]

Think about the life and conversion of Paul (Saul). He was accused of persecuting Jesus. "Saul, Saul, why persecuteth thou me?" The 'me' being Jesus (Acts 9:4). For this, he was forgiven, but if he had deliberately chosen to resist (kick against his call on that Damascus Road) that would have been sin against the Holy Spirit.

This condemnation is not something God, Jesus, nor the Holy Spirit desires. It is the end result brought upon those by themselves who don't believe and/or reject Jesus, even though the Holy Spirit has made it possible for them to "see" and be aware of who Jesus is. The unpardonable sin then is more than "a Christian theological concept," as it is often defined. It is a judgmental reality that when anyone refuses to accept even the possibility of salvation (by way of repentance) that one blocks forgiveness, and ultimately blocks one's self out from the blessings of knowing and living for Jesus, in this world and the world to come.

> *For this is good and acceptable in the sight of God our Savior; Who will have all (people) to be saved, and come unto the knowledge of truth* (I Timothy 2:3-4).

CHAPTER TWELVE

NEGATIVITY AND THE POWER THEREOF

In September of 1999, I spent three weeks ministering in Itarsi, India. Itarsi is the central most city in India. Other than that, it's not known for much, except for how one Christian family gave the city religious prominence. For better than fifty years, a diminutive but powerfully anointed Pentecostal preacher by the name of Dr. Kurian Thomas preached, prayed, worshipped, and taught about the Gospel of Jesus Christ even when the predominately Hindu culture sought to silence him. After much travail, he, his wife, their five sons and one daughter eventually gained the respect of the community, primarily because of Dr. Thomas' desire to extend missions to young, less fortunate men. It wasn't long before a Pentecostal church was established, a college was developed, and a seminary started. Today, some seventy years later, the Pentecostal Church of Itarsi is vibrant and strong, two colleges (one for young men and the other for young women) instructs a combined enrollment of 200 students annually, and the seminary continues to prepare young men for evangelism throughout India and beyond.

Dr. Kurian Thomas and his wife went to be with the Lord in 2000 and 2004, respectively. Four of their sons, Drs. George, Sam, Abraham, and Jacob Thomas are here, in the United States. The fifth son, Dr. Matthew Thomas commutes between the United States and India, spending six months in each country, from year to year. They also have a daughter, Mary, who also lives in the states. The six months that Matthew is in India, he spends leading the work first founded by his father. It was through an invitation extended by him that I first went to India.

While there that September, I was privileged to experience what I call "religion in the raw." To a great extent, the practicing of our Christian faith is clouded by our education, materialism, traditions, and other factors. Such have a tendency to get in the way of, for example, the authentic miracle working power of the Spirit. We have erected so many layers that it's all we can do to communicate the Gospel with clarity and power. I found that the worship experiences, especially, were void of such trappings and bordered on being refreshingly primitive. The fervor and intensity of all was even further heightened because of the very real attacks from outsiders who are offended by Christianity. It's an experience that's best witnessed and difficult to articulate.

After almost three weeks, I'd preached seven sermons at the church and taught better than forty hours in the college and in the seminary. The day that I was to begin my journey home, including a three hour drive over mostly rural and unpaved roads to get to the domestic airport in New Delhi, in order to fly to the international airport in Mumbai (formerly Bombay); then to London, England, and subsequently to the United States (i.e. New York), I vividly recall having my bags packed and ready to go around 8:30 that morning. Having been not just away, but essentially living in another "world," only increased my anxiousness to return home. I'd obviously missed my wife and my sons, and as the cliché goes, "Be it ever so humble, there's no place like home." As I awaited the knock on the door of my rather spacious dormitory style room I'd been living in, that was a part of the Thomas' residence and for a few days shared with other ministers and/or teachers who'd come from the United States, as well, I could hear the heavy rain falling on the roof, as the room was on the second floor.

When Satché, one of the students, knocked on my door, I opened it with suitcases in tow. "Dr. Carter," he said, in his native accent, "you cannot leave now… driver said that the roads are washed out. You must wait. All of the students wait for you at college. Dr. Thomas said that you can come teach." My suitcases that a moment earlier seemed light, now suddenly felt much heavier. I couldn't believe I was in a holding pattern, and I wasn't even flying. Not to mention, I was requested to go to the college, a little less than a hundred yards away, and teach. Teach what? I'd taught practically everything I knew, and my brain and my spirit had all but checked out in anticipation of going home.

Reluctantly, as Satché waited for me, I unpacked my sandals, put them on—no need getting my loafers soaked and muddied—and while he held an umbrella, we jogged our way through the rain, down one street, turning at the corner, then down another, to the college.

Roughly sixty young men from each of the classes were cramped into one of the humid classrooms. A good number of them stood around the walls and in the rear. It was as though this was some planned program that those present that day were told not to miss. The windows were half-opened, held up by sticks and other props, while the blades of the Casablanca style ceiling fan whipped the beaded pull-string into a swirl. The room seemed hazy, as through the cloudy atmosphere outside had crept inside. It was almost surreal.

I had no idea what I would say to these prospective preachers, pastors, and evangelists. I had no notes, and in my reluctance to come, I didn't even have my Bible. Of course, I had taught some of them, but this was an assembly of sorts. I had seen most of them, in worship and around the college, but most of my teaching was relegated to the upper classmen and the seminary (Master's degree) students. In fact, many of the underclassmen knew little English, which meant I would need an interpreter.

In a moment of inspiration, having caught my breath, and having greeted everyone, I picked up a piece of that round, one inch, "Little House on the Prairie," dusty chalk and drew the biggest cross I could on the old fashioned slate (black) board, as I stood at the front of the class. The hum of their chatter ceased. They were extremely respectful, and there was also the sense that they didn't want to miss anything.

Having wiped the chalk residue off of my right hand and arm, I turned to them and asked, "What is the importance of this symbol?" A hand was raised, then another, and then another. Answers—good and correct answers—were being given and briefly discussed: "the cross is the symbol of our Christian faith. The cross is God's ultimate love, stretching wide for all humanity, and reaching high from earth to heaven. The cross is the symbol of our salvation, on which the Son of God suffered, bled, and died for our sins." "Good answers," I'd say, "But I'm still looking for something that I haven't heard, yet. So, allow me to rephrase my question. What is the importance of the cross in relationship to servanthood?"

They briefly whispered to each other. Then, one upperclassman quoted (you know) *"Greater love hath no one than this that a man lay down his life for his friends"* (St. John 15:13). "You're saying then that the cross is about sacrifice?" I asked. Most of them, including the one who'd given this answer, sheepishly shook their heads. (It took me a while to get used to it, but by-in-large, Indians—at least these Indians—shook their heads side to side to indicate yes, and they nod their heads up and down to indicate no. It can be very disconcerting.) He was close. They were close.

Finally, another hand slowly went up from the rear corner, near the door. It was Satché's hand. Satché was a lovable college junior. Although practically all of the students came from difficult and impoverished backgrounds, they were extremely bright and intelligent. Satché, however, seemed to struggle, and his college mates knew it. So, they often poked fun at him, especially since Dr. Thomas had basically made him his errand boy. Whenever the president, Dr. Thomas, needed hot water for tea, Satché would get it. If paper was needed for the fax or copier machine, Satché would replace it, inasmuch as there was no secretary. So, when everyone realized that Satché was about to respond, it was as though a collective, "Yeah, right. This is going to be good" sarcasm filled the room, as all were in anticipation of a good belly laugh.

"I will tell you, Dr. Carter. I will tell you the answer. The importance of the cross and what it means about servanthood is that Jesus did not come down." I thought I would burst! However long my delay was, it was immediately forgotten as sunshine broke through that cloudy room. It was better than when the character Jamal Malik gave his final answer in the Oscar winning movie, Slumdog Millionaire.

What does it really mean to be a servant? Obedience. Submissiveness. Loyalty. Discipline. Again, all of the aforementioned are good and correct. Notwithstanding, Jesus uniquely personifies the response I prefer, as we look to him, our greatest example of what it means to be a servant.

The writer of Ecclesiastes wrote, "... *the race is not to the swift, nor the battle to the strong...*" (9:11). Jesus taught as recorded in Mark, "... *but he that shall endure to the end, the same shall be saved*" (13:13), and John wrote, "...*When Jesus knew that his hour was come that he should depart out of this world unto the Father, having loved his own which were in the world, he loved them unto the end*" (13:1). Then, the writer of Hebrews wrote to the church, "... *and let us run with patience the race that is set before us*" (12:1). There is, in the deeper understanding of servanthood, not only the aspects and attitudes of self denial and faithfulness, but of endurance. And, that such endurance is for the greater good of the Gospel, so that God will be glorified.

It is what Jesus did not do, during His earthly ministry, during His passion, and during specifically His crucifixion that claims our attention. Having been baptized and led by the spirit into the wilderness, Jesus prayed and fasted for forty days. Having done so, he became hungry, and that's when Satan showed up to tempt him (St. Matthew 4: 1-11). Each of Satan's three temptations were enticing, but Jesus refused in order to affirm his servanthood.

Then, three years later, He would agonize in the Garden of Gethsemane, praying and begging God to remove Him from his assignment. It was during this tremendous struggle that we find the most glorious and profound words of negativity ever spoken—one in particular—*"Father, if thou be willing, remove this cup from me:* **nevertheless** *not my will, but thine, be done."* Although there's an implied sense of resignation, there is also a greater sense of resistance. And, although Jesus is speaking to his Father, I cannot help but think He is also saying to Satan, "never!" It was at that moment when God sent an angel to strengthen Jesus, as he prayed "more earnestly: sweating great drops of blood." (St. Luke 22:42-44). Servanthood isn't servanthood without a **nevertheless.**

Finally, we come to the cross, on Calvary. As Jesus hung from the cross, taunts and mockers tempted Him to abort His assignment. They didn't realize how far He'd already come in order to get to where He was. It would have been ludicrous to abandon the assignment at that moment so close to completion. Yet, how often is that our most vulnerable moment? Pain has set it. Weakness seems to prevail. Other options look good. As another saying goes, "It's always darkest before it's dawn."

> *If thou be the Son of God, come down from the cross.... He saved others; himself he cannot save. If he be the King of Israel, let him now come down from the cross, and we will believe him. He trusted God; let him deliver him now* (St. Matthew 27:40b, 42-43a).

A servant of God has power, but such power is never for exhibitionism. It is for fulfilling our mandate, our call, and our assignment. Exhibitionists use power to promote themselves and for the short term. Servants use power to witness God and endure. Jesus had the power. He had the power to come down. He had the power to end the whole horrible scene on that hill. He could have summoned angels to rescue him. He could have wiped out every soldier and enemy. But, he didn't. He did not come down. Praise God. Hallelujah. As the song says, "He would not come down from the cross just to save Himself. He decided to die just to save me."

It would have taken some power to quit prematurely...to come down, but it took more power not to come down. Our salvation is met, because He did not come down.

It was because Jesus was crucified and that He did not come down from the cross that after three horrible and excruciating hours the Gospel writer John wrote:

> *When Jesus therefore had received the vinegar, he said, It is finished: and he bowed his head and gave up the ghost. But when they (the soldiers) came to Jesus, and saw that he was dead already.* (19: vss. 30 and 33a).

John further indicated that a man by the name of Joseph (of Arimathaea and a disciple of Jesus) went to Pilate, the governor of Judea and Samaria, who had come to Jerusalem for the Passover Feast, and asked him for permission to bury Jesus' body. Interestingly, another man, named Nicodemus, first mentioned in the fourth chapter, joined Joseph, bringing various burial spices. Together, they took the body of Jesus, wrapped it in linen clothes with the spices and placed Jesus' body in a new tomb, in the garden area where Jesus was crucified (vss. 38-42, my summary and paraphrase).

What is the core or central message of the Good News that saves us, that we teach and preach, and that we're called to use in winning souls to Jesus Christ? In essence, the message of the Good News is that Jesus Rose From the Dead! In order to get to that, however, is the belief in the resurrection narratives found in the New Testament gospels.

All four gospels affirm that on the first day of the week (Sunday), in the early morning, that Jesus was raised from the dead. However, let the record show that the resurrection of Jesus is told based on negatives. How interesting, but not surprising. The Gospel writer Luke wrote: *"And they* (presumably the women referred to on Luke 23:55 and possibly Joseph of Aramithaea [51]) *entered in* (the tomb) *and found not the body of the Lord Jesus"* (vs. 3). Still further, *"He is not here, but is risen"* (vs. 6a). The Gospel writer Matthew wrote, *"And the angel... said unto the women, Fear not ye: for I know that ye seek Jesus, which was crucified. He is not here...Come, see the place where the Lord lay."* (28: 5&6) Likewise the Gospel writer Mark simply, yet, profoundly wrote, *"He is not here."* (16:6)

Whether we have ever considered it, or not, the very foundation of our Christian faith is based on the words HE IS NOT HERE, or the belief in "the empty tomb." Permit me to return to a previous thought about pessimism. In chapter two, I mentioned that one can be pessimistic and still have hope. Such seems counter to the general and accepted psychology associated with the understanding of personality traits, for example, how one may view the water in the glass. Some see the glass half filled, which is supposed to mean that one is positive and optimistic, while others see the glass as half empty, which is supposed to mean that one is negative and pessimistic.

When it comes to my faith, it is rooted and grounded in, do I dare postulate, the glass being half empty? And, even more it is based on...**empty...the empty tomb.** From this point of view, the pessimism is well founded and appreciated, and such is the power of negativity.

And, there is more. Or, shall I say that there are more no's...more negatives that give us pessimistic hopefulness. Indeed, I won't even comment further or even dare editorialize. I simply invite you to appreciate and contemplate with me in the sublime nature of the following words that inform us on what not to expect in our eternal home:

> *...For the first earth and the first heaven were passed away; and there was no more sea.... And God shall wipe away all tears from their eyes; and there shall be no more death, neither sorrow, nor crying, neither shall there be any more pain: for the former things are passed away.*

> *And there shall be no more curse....And there shall be no night there; and they need no candle, neither light of the sun* (Revelation 21:1b & 4; 22:3a & 5).

"**B**ecause thou hast seen me,
thou hast believed: blessed are they that
have not seen, and yet have believed."
-St. John 20:29

NOTES

Chapter 1: Negativity and God's Law

1. Walter J. Harrelson, *The Ten Commandments For Today*, Louisville, Westminster John Knox Press, 2006, pg. 21.
2. Ibid., pg. 18.
3. Harrelson, pg. 3.
4. Ibid., pg. 21.

Chapter 2: Negativity and Evolution In Brief

1. R. Vork, Personality & Social Psychology Bulletin, September, 2007.
2. R.R. Baumeister, "Bad Is Stronger Than Good," *Review of General Psychology*, 2001.
3. Baumeister.

Chapter 3: Negativity and Slowing Things Down

1. Charles F. Stanley, *Landmines In the Path of the Believer*, Nashville, Thomas Nelson, 2007, pg. 227.
2. Tom Benjamin, *It's All In Your Mind*, Indianapolis, IN, Vision International Publishing, 2008, pg. 189.
3. Harold A. Carter, *The Freedom of Obedience*, San Bernadino, CA., Here's Life Publishers, Inc. (unpublished), 1982, pg. 8.

The Freedom of Obedience is a manuscript that to date remains unpublished. It was only during the process of my writing this book that my father, Dr. Carter, made me aware that more than 25 years ago, he was in the process of publishing a similar work and let me read it. To say the least, I was totally amazed and still remain so, as to the similarity of thought. I am honored to include this resource as a reference.

Chapter 4: Negativity and The One Word Boundary

1. Adam Hamilton, *Seeing Gray in a World of Black and White*, Nashville, Abingdon Press, 2008, pg. 151.
2. Henry Cloud and John Townsend, *Boundaries*, Grand Rapids, Michigan, Zondervan, 1992, pg. 71.
3. Ibid., pg. 70.
4. Ibid., pg. 71.
5. Cloud., pg. 71.
6. Amanda Hinnant, 10 Ways to Say No, Guilt Free, The Bigger Picture-Your Life-MSN Lifestyle, March, 2009
7. Cloud, pgg. 49-50.
8. Ibid., pg. 50.
9. Ibid., pg. 51.
10. Cloud, pgg.52-53.
11. Kenneth S. Wuest, *Word Studies in the Greek New Testament*, Grand Rapids, Michigan, Wm. B. Eerdmans Publishing Company, 1973, pg. 79.
12. Wuest, pg. 79.
13. Harold A. Carter, *The Freedom of Obedience*, San Bernadino, CA, Here's Life Publishers, Inc. (unpublished), 1982, pg. 7.

Chapter 5: Negativity and God's Stop Sign

1. Walter J. Harrelson, *The Ten Commandments for Today*, Louisville, Westminster John Knox Press, 2006, pg. 22.
2. Kenneth S. Wuest, *Word Studies in the Greek New Testament*, Grand Rapids, Michigan, Wm. B. Eerdmans Publishing Company, 1973, pg. 76.
3. Charles F. Stanley, *Landmines In the Path of the Believer*, Nashville, Thomas Nelson, 2007, pg. 228.

4. Tom Benjamin, *It's All In Your Mind*, Indianapolis, IN, Vision International Publishing, 2008, pgg. 66-67.

Chapter 6: Negativity and A Society Without Regrets

1. U.S. Department of Justice/FBI's Web Site, Crime in the U.S., 2005.
2. Thomas L. Friedman, *The New York Times*: Swimming Without A Suit (Op-ed), April 2009.
3. Jon Meacham, *Newsweek:* The End of Christian America, April, 2009. (issue date, magazine, April 13).
4. Ibid.

Chapter 7: Negativity and Disliking What God Dislikes

1. *Vine's Complete Expository Dictionary*, Nashville, TN, Thomas Nelson Publishers, 1985, pg. 113.
2. *Websters II New Riverside University Dictionary*, Boston, MA, The Riverside Publishing Company, 1984.
3. Vine's., pg. 113.
4. Waldo Beach, *Christian Ethics in the Protestant Tradition*, Atlanta, John Knox Press, 1988, pg. 45.
5. Adam Hamilton, *Seeing Gray in a World of Black and White*, Nashville, TN, Abingdon Press, 2008, pg. 147.
6. Walter J. Harrelson, *The Ten Commandments For Today*, Louisville, Westminister John Knox Press, 2006, pg. 22.

Chapter 8: Negativity and Doing Without

1. John F. Baggett, *Seeing Through the Eyes of Jesus*, Grand Rapids, Michigan, William B. Eerdmans Publishing Co., 2008, pg. 109.

Chapter 9: Negativity and Unanswered Prayer

1. Alice Cullinan, *The Star*: "Why God Sometimes Says 'No,'" N.C. Cleveland Co., 2009.

Chapter 10: Negativity and the First Psalm

1. Eugene H. Peterson, *The Message*, Colorado Springs, Colorado, Navpress, 2002, pg. 912.
2. John Phillips, *Exploring the Psalms, Volume One*, Neptune, New Jersey, Loizeaux Brothers, 1988, pg. 16.
3. Phillips, pg. 18.
4. Martin Patriquin, *Macleans*: Maclean's Interview, Canada, April, 2009, pg. 17.
5. Phillips, pg. 18

Chapter 11: Negativity and The Unpardonable Sin

1. Tim Demy and Gary Steward, *101 Most Puzzling Bible Verses*, Eugene, Oregon, Harvest House Publishers, 2006, pg. 95.
2. Henry M. Morris, *The Defender's Study Bible*, Iowa Falls, Iowa, World Publishers, 1995.
3. F. F. Bruce, *Answers to Questions*, Grand Rapids, Michigan, Zondervan Publishing House, 1973, pg. 46.
4. Demy, pg. 96.

BIBLIOGRAPHY

Baggett, John F., *Seeing Through the Eyes of Jesus*,
Grand Rapids, Michigan, William B. Eerdmans Publishing
Company, 2008.

Baumeister, R.R., *Bad Is Stronger Than Good/ Review
of General Psychology*, 2001.

Beach, Waldo, *Christian Ethics in the Protestant
Tradition*, Atlanta, John Knox Press, 1988.

Benjamin, Tom, *It's All In Your Mind*, Indianapolis,
IN, Vision International Publishing, 2008.

Bruce, F.F., *Answers to Questions*, Grand Rapids,
Michigan, Zondervan Publishing House, 1973.

Carter, Harold A., *The Freedom of Obedience*, San
Bernadino, CA, Here's Life Publishers, Inc., (unpublished),
1982.

Cloud, Henry and Townsend, John, *Boundaries*, Grand
Rapids, Michigan, Zondervan, 1992.

Cullinan, Alice, *Why God Sometimes Says 'No,'* The
Star, N.C., Cleveland, Co.,

Demy, Tim and Stewart, Gary, *101 Most Puzzling
Bible Verses*, Eugene, Oregon, Harvest House
Publishers, 2006.

Hamilton, Adam, *Seeing Gray in a World of Black and*

White, Nashville, Abingdon Press, 2008.

Harrelson, Walter J., *The Ten Commandments For Today*, Louisville, Westminster John Knox Press, 2006.

Hinnant, Amanda, *10 Ways to Say No, Guilt Free*, MSN Lifestyle, 2009.

Meacham, Jon, Newsweek, *"The Decline and Fall of Christian America,"* Harlan, IA, April 2009, Vol. CLIII, Number 15.

Morris, Henry M., *The Defender's Study Bible*, Iowa Falla, Iowa, Word Publishers, 1995.

Patriquin, Martin, *Macleans* "Mark on the Move" (Interview of Br. Gaston Deschamps), Canada, April, 2009, Vol. 122, Number 12.

Peterson, Eugene H., *The Message*, Colorado Springs, Colorado Newpress, 2002.

Phillips, John, *Exploring the Psalms, Volume One*, Neptune, New Jersey, Loizeaux Brothers, 1988.

Stanley, Charles F., *Landmines In the Path of the Believer*, Nashville, Thomas Nelson, 2007.

Vonk, R., *Personality & Social Psychology Bulletin*, 1993.

Wuest, Kenneth S., *Word Studies in the Greek New Testament*, Grand Rapids, Michigan, Wm. B. Eerdmans Publishing Company, 1973.

ABOUT THE AUTHOR

Dr. Harold A. Carter, Jr.
Pastor, New Shiloh Baptist Church

... is a third generation preacher of the Gospel of Jesus Christ, having been licensed and ordained in the church of his upbringing (1980), the New Shiloh Baptist Church, Baltimore, Maryland.

... is married to Rev. Monique T. Carter, and they are the parents of two sons, Daniel Nathan and Timothy Alphonso. He is the son of Dr. and Mrs. (Also Dr.) Harold A. Carter and has one sister, Weptanomah Davis.

... is a graduate of Eastern College, St. Davids, Pennsylvania, earning a B.A. in English Literature/Writing and Religion...is a graduate of the Lancaster Theological Seminary, Lancaster, Pennsylvania, earning a Master of Divinity degree...is a graduate of the United Theological Seminary, Dayton, Ohio, earning the

Doctor of Ministry degree, and among many honors and awards, he received the Doctor of Divinity degree from the Virginia Seminary and College, Lynchburg, Virginia, and the Doctor of Humane Letter from Cumberland College, Williamsburg, Kentucky. In 2006, he was inducted into Morehouse College, Atlanta, Georgia, as a Martin Luther King, Jr. Distinguished Preacher.

... is the pastor (since 1996) of the New Shiloh Baptist Church, Baltimore, Maryland, serving along with his father, Dr. Harold A. Carter. Together, they lead the congregation of more than 5,000 active members with emphasis on Missions, Evangelism, and Christian Education. His preaching is heard widely throughout this nation, and through radio, television and internet streaming broadcasts. He formerly pastored the First Baptist Church, Petersburg, Virginia, believed to be the oldest African-American Baptist congregation in America* (1989-1996) and the Zion Baptist Church, Reading, Pennsylvania (1983-1989).

... his ministry has taken him to such places as the Middle East, Romania, Panama, Trinidad, Korea, China, England, the Bahamas, and India, where he has also been privileged to share the Gospel. He sees his "call" to the ministry as "The Divine compulsion to do God's will."

... he has served on a number of boards and conferences. Presently, he serves as the Vice-President and New Testament/ Hermeneutics Professor for the Determined Biblical & Theological Institute of Baltimore, Maryland. He is also a Co-Mentor for doctoral candidate students at the United Theological Seminary, Dayton, Ohio. Additionally, he is the Co-chair of the Board of Directors of the New Shiloh Village Development

Project, a non-profit organization with a goal of community development, including the New Shiloh Senior Living building (an 81-unit facility).

... as an outgrowth of his ministry, publications include: *Jesus is Knocking at Your Door, Six Significant Sermons, The Sacred Marriage— Getting Started in Pastoral Ministry, The Burning Bush,* (co-author), and *Harold's Hermeneutics: Volume One.* Additionally, he has written several songs, three of which have been recorded and performed by New Shiloh's Music Ministry, entitled "You Will Know," "I Never Shall Forget to Praise Your Name," and "Always."

*Woodson, Carter G., *The Story of the Negro Retold*, The Associated Publishers, Inc., Washington, D.C., 1945, pg. 62.

Made in the USA